Daring to Be Different:
A Manager's Ascent to Leadership

by

James A. Hatherley

PUBLISHING COMPANY

Star
PUBLISHING COMPANY

Publisher   *Stuart Hoffman*
Production by Shepherd, Inc.
Cover Design   *Donna Lenox*
Project Coordination   *Jana Sheldon*

For information about our products, call (650) 591-3505 or visit our website:
www.starpublishing.com

ISBN 0-89863-266-8

To arrange for bulk purchase discounts for corporate training, sales promotions, premiums,
or fund-raisers, please contact the publisher at the above address.

Library of Congress Cataloging-in-Publication Data

Hatherley, James A., 1947–
    Daring to be different : a manager's ascent to leadership / by James A. Hatherley.
        p.   cm.
    ISBN 0-89863-266-8 (alk. paper) -- ISBN 0-89863-270-6 (alk. paper)
    1. Leadership. 2. Management. I. Title.
    HD57.7.H389 2003
    658.4'092--dc22   2003060394

Printed in the United States of America
10 9 8 7 6 5 4 3 2 1   03 04 05 06 07 08 09

Contents

Preface

I don't know who records such information, or confirms its accuracy, but somewhere along the way I have heard that over 90 percent of all *management books* are not read from cover to cover. If this is true, you have to wonder why so many *management books* are purchased each year despite repeatedly failing to sustain the attention of their readers for the duration of the author's advice and counsel.

It was within this context that I wrote *Daring to Be Different, A Manager's Ascent to Leadership.* Actually, the inspiration to write this book came from the people who have worked for me over the years, who have been the consumers of numerous management approaches, and convinced me that my approach was different.

While it is certainly flattering to receive such feedback, it is also challenging to understand and explain what this *difference* is all about, and even more challenging to convey to prospective readers why this book about *being different* is a better, and hopefully more valuable option for them than the available alternatives. A few of my objectives in meeting these challenges were to:

- Provide material that is easy to read, easy to remember, and easy to use.
- Avoid telling war stories that suggest my experiences are your experiences when we all know they are not.
- Refrain from telling you what you must do.
- Use metaphors and examples that enable you to critically think and ultimately understand and decide what you need to do; providing a little irreverence and humor in the process.

- Provide tools that will help you transition from manager to leader.
- Write a book that managers value as so practical and relevant to their business that they subsequently order copies for their aspiring leaders.

As a manager for over 25 years, I know that leading is an ongoing and evolving process in which even the most experienced managers must continue to learn and relearn if they are to effectively lead their organizations. My book was written with this personal bias. At the same time, however, as a parent of two postgraduate leaders-in-training, I could not resist providing mentored guidance for new managers just starting out.

Daring to Be Different has already become a valuable addition to courses where innovation and leadership are taught. In fact, many managers-to-be are being introduced to my book as supplemental reading in business courses at colleges and universities. I commend their instructors for *being different* by going beyond the typical management textbooks!

By the time you have finished reading the final page you will realize this story is about you. It is about your willingness and ability to break the paper handcuffs of conformity and take personal control of your circumstances; taking the required action to move forward in your life and to ascend to greater heights in your career.

Success is seldom a matter of luck. The anecdotes and metaphors in my book will provide the inspiration, however, you must provide the perspiration to make the difference. Best of success!

Jim Hatherley
Boston, MA

Acknowledgments

So much goes into the writing of a book that it is impossible to completely do it alone. This is certainly true with my book. Therefore, it is with thanks and gratitude that I would like to offer several personal acknowledgments.

The first place to begin is the special people with whom I have worked through the years. Many of my colleagues have repeatedly encouraged me to "write a book" that would use my stories, analogies, and theories to help others develop a "different" management style and more motivational leadership practices. While certainly flattering, left to myself there most certainly would have been no book.

However, over time their collective encouragement merged into a single, but irresistibly persuasive voice, urging me to give it a try. I'm glad that I finally relented and heard the message. Writing this book, with all the personal reflection that has gone into it, has been an extraordinary gift.

When you think about it, the passion, motivation, and trust derived from your colleagues are the most important endorsements that any author writing about leadership can receive. Their voice has both guided me and been the emotional and philosophical "wind beneath my wings" every step along the way. I am grateful for that confidence and their selfless support.

It is also important to receive feedback and directional comments from leaders who are actively involved in the daily operations of their own organizations. To that extent, I especially appreciated the time and guidance provided by Jim Smith, Chairman and CEO of First Health, and Ed Longo, President of Decision Consultants, Inc. Their helpful insights are woven through the chapters of the book. And, Jack Hayes, who recently retired from UPS after a distinguished career, honors me every time he tells the caribou story, which he has elevated to an art form.

I also want to acknowledge Paul Szep, twice recipient of the Pulitzer Prize for editorial cartooning while at the Boston Globe, who graciously depicted my likeness as a "12-point buck," without completely destroying my image.

And, acknowledgments would be incomplete without thanking my family for enduring this project and providing their encouragement. I think Reene is still impressed that anyone could be consistently coherent between 3 AM – 5 AM when I did much of my writing. And, Scott and Christine, who both contributed to, and lived out many of the stories, are even more impressed that people will pay for the same advice that I have been trying to give them for years.

Thanks also to Prudence Horne who was often more excited about the prospects for my book than I.

CHAPTER 1

You Don't Get To Be A 12-Point Buck By Luck!

"The intention of this book is concentrated on providing a different path, with more passionate and subtle tones, for those managers who feel trapped within the box of uncomfortable conformity."

"The better you are, the luckier you get."

We have a lot in common:

- We all have "bosses."
- We are, at various times, fascinated, frustrated, motivated and annoyed by their behavior, frequently all in the same day.
- We often use the words "my boss" at the beginning of a sentence to explain the unexplainable, to rationalize the irrational, or to evoke a measure of shared sympathy, consolation, or understanding from others having similar experiences with their own bosses.
- We continually talk about "what we would have done differently if we were the boss" (but are often secretly happy that we are not).

However, we also have in our mind the blurred image of a manager who suddenly sweeps onto the scene like a paragon of leadership, whose passion and inspiration make us jump out of bed each day, and even look forward to Monday morning.

The question for many of us is "How do we get to be that kind of leader?"

Born Followers?

However, is it possible that only certain people are born to be leaders? Has destiny encrypted special leadership genes within the DNA of the chosen few, leaving too little left for everyone else?

While the concept is highly doubtful, people talk about "born leaders" all the time. It's probably more of a rationalization expressed by people who are attracted to leaders, yet fear the notion and the responsibility of actually leading. After all, if the select few are born to be leaders, it's easy for everyone else to think of themselves as "born followers," or to simply rationalize that leading comes down to luck and that some people just have more of it than others.

However, in the process they forget one of life's little maxims: "The better you are, the luckier you get." Unfortunately, those who see themselves as chronically "unlucky" never seem to make the reverse connection.

The confusion may arise from the often observed paradox of leadership. Since most managers struggle at leading, and look bad in the process, an effective leader appears even more naturally suited for the role, perhaps even making it "look easy," similar to an accomplished pianist or a master teacher. Yet, people seldom say that a person is a born pianist or born teacher. Why then a "born leader"?

Perhaps the more important question is that even if it were true that there are "born leaders," why are too few of them apparently being born?

The Metamorphic Leader?

Nor are leaders formulaically "made," as if just anyone can be placed into a developmental machine or inserted into a business model, or sent to a training program and metamorphically emerge as an effective leader. As improbable as this is, corporations attempt to do it every day. People are appointed as managers and are expected to lead, as if it were as natural as breathing and just as easy. Most are good people and dedicated employees. However, until they are able to take the conscious steps necessary to seize the leadership initiative, the majority of managers end up being poor leaders no matter how big their office, how much they are paid, how much training they get, or even who they know.

Discouraged by their failure to develop leaders on their own, some corporations believe they can bypass the developmental process by attracting higher degreed candidates, with even higher salaries, assuming that they have "mastered" the science of leading in graduate school. This incomprehensibility reminds me of one of my fraternity brothers who had a date that was a sure thing to result in his first sexual experience.

Like most college students at the time, he studied for the event by going to the library and reading up on the process. After memorizing the diagrammatic model of the female erogenous zones, and the nine steps to effective love making, he was ready. However, at the moment of truth, he discovered to his dismay that his date did not have the programmatic lines and identifying numbers on her body parts that he had memorized. He became quickly confused, could not adapt, failed to execute, and as a result did not get "lucky"!

The lesson is obvious. "Real life" is typically far more complicated and far less forgiving than the canned "case study" world of the classroom, but far more relevant and longer lasting. People get hurt, fortunes are lost, lives are changed, and careers are destroyed every day by managers who fail to lead. Sadly, few regrets are ever expressed, most likely because bad managers are either too oblivious to recognize their inadequacies, too self-absorbed to realize their missteps, or just in denial of their responsibility for their failures.

The 12-Point Buck

Here's another valuable lesson that I will never forget. I learned it when dropping my son off at Cornell University in Ithaca, New York, a beautiful school offering a degree in Hotel Management despite being located in a city offering too few hotels to accommodate visiting parents.

Unable to get a room close to campus, I was finally able to get a reservation in a bed and breakfast hunting lodge, ten miles out of town and well off the beaten path. It was not a great place, but it was owned by a woman whose understanding exceeded her appearance. As she was making breakfast, she mentioned that a party of hunters would be checking in later in the day. I wondered why they were attracted to her property. She told me that her land was quite large and that there was a 12-point buck "out back" that was the real attraction. When I asked if she was concerned that a hunter would shoot the meal ticket animal, her reply was unforgettable. "Honey," she laughed, "I don't worry about him. You don't get to be a 12-point buck by luck!"

People Want To Be Led, Not Managed

And, that, of course, is the point. Leaders are not born, nor are they programmatically engineered, nor academically produced from MBA programs. All the wishing and hoping and planning and scheming in the world will not produce a leader. Effective leaders are people who have the ability to merge their talent, vision, ambition, and passion to successfully guide their teams (and themselves) within the framework of their organization's strategy and to fulfill the objectives of their mission.

They also understand a few key principles regarding their followers:

- They do not purposely intend to do a bad job.
- They do want to be acknowledged for doing a good job.
- They would prefer to like, even admire, their bosses—but trust is a more important attribute.
- They want a personal connection to their leaders.
- They want to be inspired, not intimidated.
- They perform better when they understand where they are going, and how they will get there.
- They feel more secure when they are led, not managed.

Therefore, there is obviously much more to leading than being born into it, reading about it, or even talking about it. If only it were that easy. Frankly, when it comes to leaders we need more visionaries with optimistically broader views. We also need fewer books from military and sports celebrities suggesting that their heroic experiences are similar to those being experienced by everyone else.

My personal experience has also shown that there is no formula for the development of an effective leadership style. Each leader's style is unique and reflects the manner and passion through which they reapply the lessons of their learning, and pass on the knowledge from their experiences that cause real people to change their behavior in the real world and under real conditions to achieve their real objectives.

In short, leading is an individualized journey, the best part of which is that all leaders are works in progress because they are continually evolving and (re)learning how to lead.

The Feel

Think about it in this context. Great chefs do not blindly and obediently follow the directions of another restaurant's recipes. They create different specialties for those who are willing, if not eager, to pay for a unique dining experience prepared from someone "lucky" enough to have been "born" with a gift for cooking (even if only acquired after years of training). Through their experiences the best chefs develop "the Feel" for their ingredients, and of their art, which gives them the confidence to become more creative and more successful.

The same is true for all effective leaders. Managers become leaders only after they develop "the Feel" for the attributes of leading which inspire the confidence and trust that their people willingly and enthusiastically follow. Development of "the Feel" begins when a manager becomes comfortable with the image they see in their mirror each morning. It happens when they gain a holistic understanding of their people, their organization, and the universe in which they compete. And it all comes together when they master the ability to skillfully orchestrate the multitude of roles and relationships within their areas of responsibility.

Managers begin to become leaders when they think about what it means to be a leader; when they are able to visualize the act of their leading; when they can understand and relate the essence of their leadership; and when they can communicate their vision to their followers in clear and comprehensible terms. They become leaders when they learn to metaphorically translate everyday images, however unconventional, into a broader perspective to which their followers can relate, and upon which they can act.

Once they gain the skills and confidence to behave like a leader, they begin to hear how they have an "inherent" ability (e.g., "the gift") to motivate and energize others to follow. But, it all begins with "the Feel," which provides the confidence that enables a manager to ascend to the loftier position of mentor-leader.

The key question, then, is "How do I get there?" The simple answer is that it is not a simple process. While you'll believe it when you feel it, if you haven't felt it yet—keep trying. A twelve point buck, even a metaphorical one, doesn't become a twelve pointer overnight, but it definitely has little to do with luck.

The Leadership Challenge

This brings us to the goals of the book—to challenge your thinking and to help you ascend from being a manager to a more self-fulfilled leader by:

- broadening your attitude about managing
- raising your awareness about leading
- providing the tools to help you make it happen.

Numerous stories and analogies will be presented as philosophical and conceptual learning (and "unlearning") tools to help managers make the transition to mentor-leader. These are leaders who are not only innately "different," but whose advice and counsel make the discernible difference in helping others to discover and expand their unique gifts while developing their own leadership points.

As the artist, in the following story, described her process, I immediately knew that she was describing what made a leader different from a manager. Managers can typically deal with what is directly in front of them and equally obvious to everyone else. However, leaders work harder to find the subtle ways that passionately express what they uniquely see and feel. Even when others have access to the same resources or share the same objectives, leaders find a way to be different.

Bold Colors and Subtle Tones

When I was in Charleston, SC a few years ago, I couldn't help but notice the large number of art galleries in the city. The majority of the paintings for sale were "street scenes" of homes and buildings in the historical area. While most of the artists' works were excellent, I kept coming back to one studio that appealed to me as having the best work. In fact, there were so many first place ribbons hanging from the ceiling moldings that they grossly reduced the amount of precious wall space to display the artist's watercolors.

When I met the artist, I was surprised to find an old woman, feeble from ongoing cancer treatment (which had claimed her hair, but did not stop her from smoking). Nevertheless, as frail as she was, her handshake was as strong as an ironworker's, and her blue eyes riveted right into mine.

She told me that I had purchased her best known piece of art. The painting was a Charleston doorway and street scene that any artist could have painted, and probably had. I asked her why this rather common appearing piece of work had been such a big seller, and why she had won virtually every art competition in South Carolina for the past 25 years. Her response was quite memorable.

She said that she began her work by painting all the bold colors first, "Because that's what everyone can see." Over the next week or two, at various times of day and night, she would revisit the scene to observe the lighting, the shadows, the noise, the activity, and the personality of the place she was memorializing.

The final act was brushing in the subtle tones which only she had experienced. While she painted all the bold colors at the scene, the subtle tones were painted in her studio, with only the impressions from her stored senses to guide her hand. These strokes expressed her unique perspective of the scene and "her passion" for what she had seen and felt, making it richer, deeper, and different from the work of other artists.

The message is clear. Whether you're selling a painting or leading an organization, your "customers" can see—and value—the difference—when you have the passion and persistence to dare to be different.

This book, therefore, does not intend to present a balanced comparison between managing and leading. There are already numerous books that define these concepts and discuss the difference between managing process and leading people; or "doing things right" vs. "doing the right thing." They describe what "everyone sees," so there is little need to further explore these basic comparisons here.

Instead, the objective of this book is concentrated on providing a different path, with more passionate and subtle tones, for those managers who feel trapped within the box of uncomfortable conformity. It is for those managers who want to escape from an environment of reacting to what everyone else sees and does, and who desire to be personally empowered to pursue what they uniquely feel. This book is for managers who need to be liberated to explore their emerging skills and to challenge their personal limits.

Most importantly, it is for those who aspire to achieve and to ascend to the more personally satisfying role of a leader.

While everyone who dares to embark on this self-fulfilling quest will not reach the full twelve points, what's to lose by taking the risk? Frankly, there's more to lose by standing on life's sidelines. Most employees will only get a warm handshake and a certificate of attendance from their boss as they walk out the door for the final time—unless they take control and make a conscious move to change their fate.

Therefore, if taking orders and marching in step are all you demand in exchange for your lifetime of work and effort, you will not need this book to achieve success. Just keep your head down and your mouth closed.

However, in the sport of business, as long as you are being paid for what you produce, you are in the game. Therefore, don't wait for an invitation to play because you are already on the field, and the game is underway.

But, be forewarned, this book is definitely not a "textbook." Leadership is not learned from a book or artfully practiced because you have attended a course or have earned a degree. Instead, it is about your gaining the skill and confidence to dare to be different. The metaphors, parables, humor, and occasional irreverence provide the relational framework and the subtle tones that you will need to think differently and make the transition from manager to leader.

While many, perhaps even most, of the stories will be memorable and provide the reader with the inspiration to lead, the perspiration part of the equation is all yours.

You must make it happen for you!

Development of a full rack of antlers begins one point at a time. If you're ready to go down a different path, and to test your personal limits, follow me.

We have a lot in common.

CHAPTER 2

Daring To Be Different

"A critical truth: When you have a horse and a cart, alignment is critical. If you want good people, have good leaders. It's pretty simple."

I enjoy managing, but what I really like most is leading. If the choice of jobs is between the place at the front of the parade or the one directly behind the Clydesdales, I want to be the one in front every time. It would even be okay if I had to wear spats to match the horses.

However, if the choice is between backing up the horses or marching as a faceless uniform in a platoon of paraders, as unglamorous as it may seem, I want to be the one with the shovel. At least that job is not totally predictable and may even offer an opportunity to develop a crowd pleasing "style," not to mention the chance to move up to a bigger job, like backing up the elephants. After all, who really wants to be an indistinguishably faceless soul, wearing clothes you don't own and taking questionable directions on the road to nowhere that nobody you know ordered you to take?

Of course, the desire to be viewed as "an individual" cannot be misinterpreted to be an open invitation to routinely disobey superiors by purposely marching out of time on every step, making everyone else look bad in the process. After all, defiance is not synonymous with leadership. Nevertheless, professional naysayers (e.g., the "not to be negative, but . . ." crowd) exist in every organization. They are not a mystery to most leaders. Nor are those who feel the chronic and annoying need to serve as "the devil's advocate," passively opposing every new idea that comes down the pike, despite having none of their own. After a while they are either discounted, or dismissed, because they bring negative energy to their organizations, and dispirit other employees in the process.

However, every manager has the responsibility to stand up and speak out in the appropriate forum when they identify a problem (the easy part) *and* can offer a well considered and practical solution (much harder). Therefore, one sign of emerging leaders is their ability—and courage—to maturely explain why a different path would be the more advantageous route for the organization to take.

"Uniform" Men And Women

Daring to be different has definite risks, but it also has its unique opportunities. A poster, hung in my office for a number of years, urges, "Don't go where the path leads, go where there is no path and blaze a trail." I am reminded of this every day. Over the years I have learned that when you veer off the beaten path and rush headlong into the thicket, you often get scratched by the thorns, suffer the discomfort of poison ivy, and risk death from a thousand mosquito bites. You may not always know exactly where you are going. However, as you begin to figure out where "you are," you also see and experience different things from everybody else.

Somewhere, off the beaten path, you discover you; and while you're "out there," you learn that it's your unique sense of perspective that makes all the difference between your being a leader or a follower. What kind of difference in perspective can the paraders have when they are all wearing the same uniform and pacing to the same drumbeat, seeing the same scenery and talking about the same things? Yet, organizations continually choose their leaders from their men and women who are in uniform, and then wonder why things don't change or improve quickly enough.

Being "different" is challenging, particularly when you want to lead the organization to a different or unfamiliar place. You must develop a coherent, consistent, and sensible philosophy; be able to passionately, persistently, persuasively, and positively communicate its value to your people; provide the reason why it is worthy of them, and be willing to accept personal accountability for its anticipated, and unanticipated, consequences.

This is a very different route from those who become "leaders" by being connected to somebody else, then blindly follow their lead down the familiar path; or the "climbers" whose unabashed ambitions, and unbashful actions exceed their aggregate skills, experience, philosophy, and intelligence; or the lifers who last long enough on their job or in the organization to be given "their turn." It doesn't take employees long to see through all of these virtual leaders.

The bottom line is that while it's harder and more personally demanding to be different, it's also more energizing and personally rewarding when you are.

"You're Different. . ."

Over the years that I have been managing, I wish that I had put aside a dollar every time that someone has told me, "You're different." I'm reasonably certain that at least some (perhaps many) of these comments were not made within a flattering context, particularly from my superiors who wanted to put a saddle on my back and make me obey. I also know that I missed the positive, though typically unspoken, meaning in that message in the early stages of my managing career.

However, along the way I began to understand that, at least to subordinates, being seen as "being different" was a good thing, particularly when compared with their prior experiences with management. After enough of them had explained what they meant, I stopped asking myself if "it" was ever going to happen for me (i.e. thinking of myself as a leader, and being viewed as one by others), and started wondering why it had taken so long to occur. Ultimately, I realized that the answer was in my mirror all along (as most answers usually are). It was more about my being ready to lead, than the desire of others to be led by me.

Funny, when I was ready to lead, they were ready to follow. What timing!

Cryptograms And Other Messages

All of this has raised a series of questions, the answers to which have perplexed me for many years. For instance, in a world filled with so many "bosses," why is it that bad managing is the norm, and good leading is the rarity? Why are bad managers tolerated and often allowed to endure, while emerging leaders are reined in and given "conform to the norm" counseling before they leave their organizations out of frustration?

What makes it even worse is when the "counseling" is so subtle that you don't even know that you're being counseled. You often need the interpretive skills of a "kremlinologist" to understand the messages hidden within the rhetoric. For instance, in my first managing assignment my manager called me into his office to review a sensitive personnel issue. He ultimately suggested that I might "want to consider" a particular course of action. A month later, he angrily demanded to know why I had disobeyed his direct orders. I can remember being surprised by his reaction before naively replying, "You asked me to consider your idea as an option. I rejected it because I thought that I had a better plan. The issue has been resolved for several weeks. Is there a problem?"

I did not understand that I was being given an order. I thought I was being given some advice and input to help me resolve an issue for which I was accountable. This was the first step to understanding that to insecure or self-centered managers, clinging to a facade of positional power and authority, rigid process, and submissive obedience are often more important than results. Sadly, many years later this tendency remains a monument to the inability of many managers to relate effectively, or provide clear and direct feedback and direction to their subordinates, or to yield their authority. Instead they deliver "messages," many of which are mixed, and most of which fly so low that they are indecipherable on the human radar scope.

Here's another example. At the Monday morning staff meeting you receive the message that there is little time to waste. Therefore, when managers confront a problem it is their responsibility to step in and resolve it. The words are familiar, "Just do it;" "Get it done;" "Put it behind you and move on." So you do. By Friday, you're being asked why you hadn't consulted with somebody who had more experience before making the call. This leaves you with two options—scratching your head and looking for a bus schedule. No wonder so many managers are afraid to make a decision. There are so many "messages" flying around that they get confused with old fashioned communication.

Management Myth: Leaders Must Have Gray Hair

Perhaps part of the explanation is that the younger generation has been told to "respect their elders" for so long that they inherently consider leading to be an older person's duty—a patriarchic rite of passage which some day will be their responsibility (but not yet). Or, perhaps they have been repeatedly told that experience is a necessary and important, if not critical, component to leading. After all, isn't gray hair a symbol of wisdom and respect?

Without any disrespect for our more tenured people, we must stop trapping people into believing that there is some sort of chronological, hierarchical, gender, or seniority-based rite of passage which must be followed, or even obeyed, as they await their "turn" to lead. You don't need gray hair or have twenty years' "experience" to lead, nor do you have to be the best at what you do to be anointed as the leader. In fact, by themselves, the presence of these qualities has little to do with leading at all.

What you do need is a leadership compass and the ability to maturely and confidently communicate your vision, values, and objectives to your organization. Through your actions (not words), you must also be able to reveal the innate sense of direction that you have learned and developed while travelling off the beaten path, and to persuade people to trust why a different path—and you—are the better options for them as well.

The People Are Good, But The Leaders Are Bad

Over the years I have learned that there is a critical truth. When you have a horse and a cart, alignment is critical. If you want good people, have good leaders. It's pretty simple. Good people are not attracted to bad leaders, nor will they remain long in their charge. It stands to reason, therefore, that organizations cannot afford ineffective leaders, yet most have more than they realize, because they take leading for granted, as if they can "appoint" a leader who will be instantly able to "lead."

In fact, most organizations under-perform because their business plans overestimate the leadership capabilities of the managers responsible for delivering the expected results. There are few better ways of showing that the "leaders" of many organizations are not as capable as the people they lead.

One reason seems clear—leading is an action word. Leaders must lead, but most managers either cannot or do not. A second reason is less obvious, but more insidious. Business is changing so rapidly that an increasingly greater amount of a manager's past experience is decreasingly relevant today, and will be even less relevant tomorrow. Those who do not keep up with the speed of their business or stay current with their challenges or are disconnected from their people become less and less relevant more quickly than they know, but not as fast as their subordinates realize and must sadly endure.

The problem usually comes down to a failure to execute—both the strategy and ineffective "leaders."

Keep The People; Fire The Manager

Here's a good example. A centralized collections processing center had the lowest revenue production results of five similar collection sites. An unproductive work force, marked by unacceptable turnover and a high rate of absenteeism, was cited by the local manager as the principle reason for the poor results. When the results did not improve, the Central Office considered eliminating the people and moving the operation elsewhere.

The manager with the best results was asked to review the lagging operation with the ultimate goal of coordinating the closure of that site and the opening of another modeled after his own. His first step was to visit the "troubled" shop to personally evaluate the situation. After interviewing the local manager and employees, and observing the processes and operations, the manager realized that the situation was far different from what he had been told. The people he had been asked to eliminate were equal to or even more capable than those in his own office. Nevertheless, their results were a problem.

The local manager, however, was completely ineffective. He was responsible for several operations but was providing no time and even less leadership to the collection processing department. He had actually redirected time consuming work from another department with worse problems to the collection department, which only dispirited the collectors and further reduced their revenue stream.

The reviewing manager's final observations and recommendations were not subtle:

- The people are good, but the manager is bad.
- Keep the people and fire the manager!

What Do You Have When Results Improve And The Only Thing That Changes Is The Manager?

As a result, the revenue collection unit was managed remotely by the visiting Collection Manager, along with his own operation, for the next three months until he could hire a replacement. During that time, visits were exchanged between his "best practice office" and the "troubled site" by key personnel. A positive consultative network was established. Within six months, the procedures and morale of the employees had been restored. In a year the collections doubled. The results were produced by the same people. The only differences were better process, improved attitudes, and a different, more supportive leader.

While this may be a single anecdote, how often is this kind of experience repeated across the business world each month of every year? Why are bad managers consistently allowed to lead good people down blind career paths as though they were in that parade marching to nowhere, but getting there fast?

So, what do you have in organizations in which the results improve, but the primary changes are managerial? You've got the emergence of leaders earning their leadership "points," and looking for increasing challenges that will grow them even more.

And, how do these "emerging" leaders know they are emerging? They'll know that they're making progress the first time someone smiles at them, shakes their hand and says, "You're different."

When that happens to you, savor that moment, and remember to put aside that dollar. It's not that the "buck" will make you rich, it's that when it comes to leading, you'll know you're not poor.

CHAPTER 3

The Leadership Paradox

"Leadership is an aphrodisiac to those being led and emotionally rewarding to those who are doing the leading."

Have you ever sat among a group of employees while they're gossiping about their bosses? It usually isn't pretty. Given the opportunity to vent, my experience at many levels of organizations has shown that most people do not have an abundance of positive things to say about their managers. They typically focus on their inability to communicate (especially to listen); or observe they are out of touch with reality, or fail to provide sufficient direction or encouragement. They marvel at their apparent lack of ability, motivation, credibility, commitment and passion.

It's enough to make anybody wonder, "How did they ever get there anyway?"

Why Is Leading So Hard To Do?

Sooner, rather than later, amid all their observations and griping, lack of leadership skills will be identified as the problem. However, their real questions are, "Why doesn't anybody in authority see through that person?" and the more critical, "Why doesn't somebody just fix it?"

Not surprisingly, if you ask the same people if they know the difference between a manager and a leader, their heads will nod knowingly, and they will even tell you the difference. A leader will be viewed as one who makes them want to come to work every morning, a manager as the person responsible for making them eager to leave every night. They will say a leader is a person who makes them feel better about themselves and the value of their work. A manager makes them feel that what they have is "a job," about which they are increasingly ambivalent.

When you ask how many people have been managed by a leader during their careers, there will be uncomfortable laughter as they recall the few (if any) managers who might meet this definition. They will even tell you who they are in your organization.

You would think that leading would be as routine to a manager as preparing a balance sheet is to a CPA. Sadly, this is not the case! There is no shortage of people who aspire to the higher paying jobs of organizations, most of which entail leadership responsibilities. Yet, there are too few who seem to be able to effectively lead. This would suggest that leading is one of life's mysteries, but this can hardly be true. If you walk around a bookstore, you will soon wander into the Business Section where there are rows and rows of Management books, many of which are even sub-categorized under Leadership, written by all the leading (at least the latest) motivators. So, "the word" is certainly out there, in volumes, either at a price you can pay or at the local library for free.

In addition to the self-improvement books, there are tens of thousands of students graduating from colleges each year with business and management degrees. Add to that the hundreds of millions of dollars that corporations rotely budget each year for management training and executive development, and you can see that there's a whole lot of learning presumably going on.

Yet, with all of this "learning" going on, why is it that leading remains such a paradox? Why is the phrase "good leader" almost an oxymoron, and why are good leaders such a rare commodity? Companies need leaders, and many aspirants seemingly desire the role and the responsibilities, if not the compensation. So, why do companies say they need leaders, then make leading so difficult to do?

Big Chairs, Little People

More than twenty-five years ago, one of the few mentor-leaders in my personal experience told me that the issue was simple to explain, "There are too many big chairs and too few big people to fill them." The larger the organization, the wider the gap.

The situation is probably worse today because the organizational structures are far less "paramilitaristic" in practice than in past generations.

Employees have been successfully "trained" by their employers to become far less loyal and much more cynical. Trust and loyalty have left the building, and they will not be returning soon. Consequently, employees no longer blindly or obediently salute the corner office because they are well aware that their positions (both the manager's and the employee's) are only as secure as the next quarter's financials. And, they are increasingly and proactively exercising their employment options to fire their employer before the employer downsizes them. It's not as bad as musical chairs, but it's no longer the "job for life" environment of the past either—for anyone.

If the difference in employee stability were not enough of a problem with which to contend, organizations also have many more moving parts now than in the past. Business issues are significantly more complex and higher risk than even just a few years ago. Organizational realities like broader spans of control and a faster moving speed of business—superimposed on the annoyingly trite, but competitively real, "doing more with less" expense control philosophy—add even more pressure to leading in the real world.

In short, within this changing environment, leading is not a casual exercise. It is not just something you wake up one day and do, at least well. Leading takes time, energy, and personal commitment. You think about leading when you are a manager, but you convert your thoughts into actions when you are a leader. However, under the circumstances of real life and in live action, too many managers are pointed in too many directions to effectively lead (and seemingly all at the same time), not necessarily because they want to, but because they must. It's either run fast or die, and that means traveling with as little baggage as possible. As a result, it's a bad time to be a manager's "straggler." You either make your "numbers" or you don't, and those who fail to achieve them are either making up a "reason" or updating their resume.

Is Leading Merely Not Dispiriting Most Of The People?

The net result is that there is a generation of managers who are so increasingly obsessed about how *they* look and who are so worried about their own survival that they have too little time, and display even less inclination, to spend on the mentoring and personnel nourishment of their staffs.

One negative consequence of this shortened developmental period is that the expectation of the work force regarding their leaders has fallen so low that "leading" can almost be defined as not dispiriting most of the people. If leading is critical to an organization, how can this be a long-term positive for companies seeking to survive, let alone claim to have a competitive advantage?

But, does this mean that managers who possess the ability to effectively lead their employees and move their organizations forward will move swiftly through their companies and assume the top positions? Not necessarily, and this raises another paradox. Controlling leaders is often like herding squirrels. Leaders tend to make their "control freak" superiors, and their peers, nervous and insecure regarding their turf. Besides, how many superiors want leaders who do not reflexively salute and mindlessly obey?

Outwardly they will disingenuously encourage up and coming leaders as having the potential "right stuff" *if* they can maintain the "appropriate focus." However, inwardly, there is often the fear of their own inadequacies or the suspicion of an ambitious "hidden agenda" that does not include them. More often it's the professional jealousy of a leader's "power" to elicit the hearts and minds, passions, performance, and loyalty from their employees that bully tactics, and even money cannot come close to matching.

In short, leadership is an aphrodisiac to those being led; and emotionally rewarding to those who are doing the leading! However, the demonstrable leadership skill of others is a threat to those whose capabilities and personal ambitions are impaired by self-doubt, insecurity, and professional jealousy. In that sense, leadership skills may really be the most highly discussed, but least trusted and least valued competency in an organization, especially when the leader is viewed as a threat by a superior.

The conclusion is simple. If leading were easy, then more people would be able to do it well. Even if they could, most leaders would readily acknowledge that leading is a risky business and the road to success is not an easy one.

A leader's ability and persistence to succeed typically must exceed the aggregate energy of the organizational resistance to their being successful. In other words, becoming an acknowledged leader is something that seldom just occurs without a lot of mental and sweat equity—and courage— along the way.

The Don Quixote Concept

But even if the road is not always an easy one, the good news is that it does not take a lot to get started as long as you understand the "Don Quixote" concept. If you have your modern day Sancho Panza and Dulcinea on your team and by your side to accompany your horse, your head, and your heart, then you've got what you need to be ready to go. However, you'll also need perseverance to overcome the adversity you'll surely encounter along the way, the vision of "what it will look and be like" when you have achieved your quest, and the ability to vividly and passionately describe why the effort is as noble and worthy as the people who make the journey with you.

But remember, even though he was ridiculed for being "different," in the end it's Don Quixote who moves the world in that glorious moment when he sings "The Impossible Dream." Everyone else is relegated to the chorus, envious that they did not have the vision to dream, let alone the courage to reach for anything that seemed impossible, or possess the stamina to achieve it.

It's hard work, but it's worth the effort.

CHAPTER 4

The Monarch And The Muralist

"Monarchs are managers, chained to the past by tradition, written and unwritten rules, manuals of procedure, the chain of command, the coefficient of friction, the lie of the ball and probably even the infield fly rule."

Here are a few basic questions regarding leading:

- Is leading merely the act of ordering what your people must do, then expecting that they will eagerly obey (even without ongoing direction)?
- Is it dependent on trickle down communications that are supposed to occur through the "chain of command" in big companies (but seldom do)?
- Can anyone be made the leader simply because the boss appoints them as the manager?
- Is leading merely an extension of the "follow the leader" playground game of our youth?

Let's face it, if leading were so easy, the leadership gap between the bosses and the bossed would be one less thing for everyone to complain about. However, like so many other things, effective leading often comes down to a matter of style. Let's consider two variations of management style that can be best described as the Monarch and the Muralist.

Monarchs are managers, chained to the past by tradition, written and "unwritten" rules, manuals of procedure, the chain of command, the coefficient of friction, the lie of the ball, and probably even the infield fly rule. Deviations from process are discouraged, as is nontraditional thinking. Communication flows in one direction because information is viewed as power and purposely withheld unless there is a "need to know." If you follow the rules and are dutifully respectful and subordinate, "success" is yours, especially if you numb your brain and remain long enough on your job to assume the position of power (thereby assuring the continuation of bad practices).

The Echo Effect

Monarchs are politically connected. They always seem to know more about office politics than they do about the changing business environment. Since theirs is a hierarchical existence, they self-perpetuate by paying daily homage to their benefactors and by being obedient, protective, and predictable. However, this behavior also creates numerous unintended consequences for them:

- They get trapped into uncomfortable positions or often must accept personal compromises created by their benefactors. As a result, they develop little forward vision, as if they are traveling on life's highway while being towed behind a tractor-trailer. This makes leading their employees virtually impossible.
- They are ultimately viewed as having their heads so far up their benefactor's butt that they almost echo when they speak. Credibility with everyone in the organization, especially their subordinates, is a losing battle.
- Everyone can tell when they're in the area because when you stand next to an outhouse long enough the smells become indiscernible.
- When something happens to their benefactor, something worse usually happens to them.

The Muralist—Mission Possible

Conversely, muralists are leaders. They have the skills and ability to express the objectives of their mission to their teams in the form of mental pictures of "what it looks like." In fact, effective muralists present their vision so vividly that their team members:

- Understand what needs to be done.
- Know their roles.
- Execute their responsibilities.
- Understand the interdependencies with project participants.
- Recognize the value of their assigned task to the mission.
- Envision success, both for the project and for themselves.

Success for muralists comes from developing mutual trust among team members, and challenging them to test the limits of their individual and collective skills. By identifying the goals of the mission, yet disavowing knowledge of all the answers, the muralist creates a sense of mutual discovery within the team. This is done within a powerful social and learning dynamic, a creative environment in which to work with clear understanding of the synergies of the moving parts, and the willingness to assume both responsibility and accountability for the result.

In this environment, the team's objective to deliver their end product is far more important than hierarchical boundaries. Team members routinely assist one another by providing practical feedback to help move their projects forward. Information is shared because it is significant and vital to the success of the effort. Communication across the organization is viewed as critical, constant, and natural because the tasks are interdependent, and require all members to produce quality work and meet their deadlines.

In short, muralists create an environment in which the whole exceeds the sum of its parts. And because participants work on holistic projects, their levels of learning expand at a faster rate, making them preferred candidates to take the lead in subsequent projects or assume leadership roles in other positions (thereby expanding the philosophy within the organization).

The monarch and the muralist:

- **Muralists** dialogue;
  monarchs dictate.
- **Muralists** empower their team and challenge their limits;
  monarchs withhold authority to act by limiting challenges and enforcing outdated controls.
- **Muralists** encourage employees to exercise their judgment and question conventional wisdom;
  monarchs discourage their work force by exorcising creativity by perpetuating traditional thinking.
- **Muralists** look forward;
  monarchs look backward.
- **Muralists** are free to find a new path;
  monarchs are trapped by the rules and the route.
- **Muralists** create an environment in which people understand what they need to do—and why;
  monarchs reign over a workplace where people are expected to do what they are told.
- **Muralists** feel the subtle tones;
  monarchs see only the bold colors.
- **Muralists** lead;
  monarchs manage.
- **Muralists** dare to be different;
  monarchs are obliged to remain the same.

Viva la différance!

CHAPTER 5

Muralists Are Not Chosen; They Choose!

"Muralists are somehow related to their ancestors who tossed tea into the harbor, took their seat in the front of the bus, dared to stand alone in front of a tank, wrote the songs that moved the world, and invented life-changing companies in their garages...They are the ones who do not have to say, 'Follow me' as they leap instinctively from their foxhole because they know their followers are right behind them, equally committed to the mission."

Since it's so much simpler for employees to just keep their heads down and their mouths shut; safer to do what they're told and not attempt anything new; and easier just to kiss an occasional monarch's ring or two to get ahead, what makes a person want to become a muralist?

Why do some people voluntarily swim against the current; dare to challenge, if not defy, authority; feel the need to place their careers at risk by being visibly independent in organizations that value obedience; or to seek out new solutions, even when unasked?

Because they must!

They are somehow related to their ancestors who tossed the tea into the harbor, took their seat in the front of the bus, dared to stand alone in front of a tank, wrote the songs that moved the world, and invented life-changing companies in their garages.

Muralists are different, and they are often the difference. They are the ones who don't need to say, "follow me" as they leap instinctively from their foxholes, covered only by their philosophy, because they know that their followers are right behind them, equally committed to the mission.

Muralists willingly accept risk and attract others similarly disposed. They do not want to be trapped in the present, let alone be trapped by the past. They often wonder who was responsible for establishing "conventional wisdom," and they challenge its current relevance.

The Faster Pace And Different Rhythm Of The Muralist's Heart

Companies need muralists more than they probably realize, and definitely more than they understand or appreciate. Fortunately, these rare and "different" people, born with a little wheel in their heart that beats at a faster pace and to a different rhythm, exist in every company. Some are waiting to be discovered, but more are watching and waiting to discover the person to whom *they* choose to be connected, whose leadership skills and passion for excellence will both challenge and liberate them.

For whatever reason, most likely a combination of heredity, family, environment, education, work experience, and life experiences, muralists *both* see and foresee things differently from most others, and typically sooner. They seldom need a road map, because they intuitively know where they have to go and what they must do. They relish the task of blazing the trail because they are most comfortable when they are off the beaten path.

Without muralists, there is little movement toward innovation and even less desire to move to the front of the competitive food chain. Without muralists, companies are resigned to perpetually stay in the same worn out rut and remain on the defensive, even as they are assailed by more highly energized competitors and unpredictable business events. In short, monarchic organizations are often so inner focused that they do not adequately evaluate the hostile forces about them, or respond timely or act decisively until their options are limited to retreat or surrender.

But give monarchs credit. Over time, they have adapted to this reality and figured out how to survive within it. They have learned how to set low expectations for their organizations, then rationalize their results and even lavishly celebrate their mediocre successes when they have been "achieved."

However, even when they understand the challenges that threaten them, without the passion and commitment of their people it is difficult for monarchs to quickly mobilize their organizations to improve their position.

Consider the riddle of the lily pads as an example.

The Lily Pads

One morning a farmer observed that a lily pad had sprung up on his pond. The following day there were two lily pads, and on the third day there were four. Since they did not seem to be doing any harm he took no action. However, the number of lily pads continued to double every day until the pond was completely covered on the thirtieth day.

On what day was the pond 50% covered by lily pads, and why is it important to understand the answer?

As you think about this riddle for a moment, consider how quickly the bottom can fall out for any organization from unforeseen events that were not detected on the corporate radar scope. This is a good example of how muralists are needed to foresee and diagnose problems, then develop and implement remedies before they become catastrophes. By quickly developing an understanding of the root causes of the challenges, and foreseeing their likely consequences—or, conversely, the positive opportunities arising from them—muralists and their teams are able to effectively and prospectively identify a range of solutions to avert danger or create a competitive advantage.

So, when was the pond 50% covered with lily pads? The answer to the riddle is that the pond was half covered on the 29th day!

The more compelling aspect of the riddle, however, is the broader understanding, and realization, that the pond was only 25% covered on the 28th day, and less than 10% covered by lilies on the 26th day. Five days before the end, less than 5% of the lily pad problem was visible. In other words, vision counts! In its absence, the damage caused by an emerging, but unchecked, "blind spot" typically occurs with increasing speed and harsh unforgiveness.

Rowers and Kayakers

While the questions involving the appropriate courses of action for both muralistic and monarchic organizations are often the same, their approaches and answers are usually different. One organization kayaks forward, seeing where they are headed. The other rows forward while looking backwards, without a clear view of where they are going. The implications are clear. Both organizations are navigating through difficult waters, but muralists are looking ahead for opportunities and looking out for predators. Monarchs have their backs to the future while searching for opportunities from where they've already been. They do not have a sense for what lies ahead because they cannot see around the corner, since they are always behind the curve.

How many businesses—and disorganized managers—are chronically in their "29th day" but don't even know it?

Muralists are not afraid to offer up their best thinking against so-called conventional wisdom, even when it involves assuming personal risk. They are not anarchists because they work within the framework of the corporate strategy, but they eagerly challenge the traditional lockstepped mentality that retards forward thinking and innovation. This is why muralists are so vital to organizations and cannot be simply viewed as messengers of bad news (e.g., "we need to spend $10,000 to rid the pond of lily pads before they become a real problem") and summarily ignored or shot. The issues do not just mysteriously disappear because nobody dared to tell the boss that they were wearing no clothes and had even less sense.

Just as importantly, however, muralists also foresee upcoming business trends and competitive opportunities based on their analysis of the data or regulatory, political, and economic trends and events—even informed intuition. Instead of learning to be obedient marchers in the parade, they have been forming different views off the beaten path. Within this context, muralists are intrapreneurial evolutionaries! As a consequence, they make monarchs nervous because they are "out of [their] control."

Muralists create the reason and opportunity to act before there is the need, or pressure, to react. They do not blindly follow the rules, but adapt them to help get things done that benefit their organization. They do not see things for what they are, as much as they envision things for what they could become with a different direction, or must become with refocused strategy and purposeful leadership!

Muralists are annoying irritants to monarchs who value blind obedience. However, blind obedience is usually the path to a "lifetime of yesterdays," and retro thinking about the good old days when the downsizing begins.

The call for changing leadership does not need to be as dramatic as Patrick Henry's appeal for liberty in colonial times, but who among us did not silently admire that common man in China who suddenly emerged from the crowd and, with the whole world watching, defied "traditional wisdom" by taking the ultimate personal risk to stand alone in front of a tank?

While others wonder what to do, muralists emerge from the crowd of mediocre managers to do what needs to be done, often uncomfortably exposed and "out there," where everyone can see what they're doing. Some people will question their wisdom for selflessly accepting the personal risk to move their organization forward, but nobody can doubt (and most silently admire) their passion.

They would even do it themselves, if only they had the courage.

CHAPTER 6

Lifters And Leaners

"Lifters matter because they elevate the value of their organizations; leaners are like matter, because they have weight and take up space."

For true muralists, however, the real challenge does not come from competing with monarchs. They are more than willing to allow them their misplaced satisfaction and faded glory of the status quo. The monarchs may be on the top of their hill, but it's often the wrong hill. Their days are numbered, because their issues always seem to be in the 29th day of the business cycle. Although they are continually trying to overcome their challenges they seldom do. Many of their wounds are self inflicted.

Instead, the challenge for muralists comes from competing within themselves to test their own personal limits to move their philosophy and their organizations forward. As a result, they typically do not have to be told what needs to be done, because they have already been thinking about "it," and are either planning how to do it, or are already in motion. And they typically get it done quickly with a small group of determined devotees ("the lifters"), who uplift their organizations and upgrade the level of individual performance, as contrasted to the slow motion monarchic meeting and committee crowd ("the leaners"), who derail progress and block opportunities.

Only lifters can successfully work within a muralistic environment since these groups are inherently small, and there is nowhere to run, nowhere to hide, and nowhere to lean. Team members are self-motivated and outer focused. Their enthusiasm is contagious. Their personal standards and accountabilities are uncompromisingly high. They have faith in their leaders, collaborate with their teammates, actively participate in the strategic planning, and are passionately committed to taking personal risk to be successful. And they are willing, eager, and self-confident to play to win in an environment where less committed employees routinely fail.

Muralists are not ambivalent when it comes to their lifters. For example:

The Starfish

There is a well-known story about a man walking along the shore at dawn. A violent storm during the night had left the beach littered with debris. In the distance he could see the image of a child silhouetted against the rising sun, racing between the sand and the water. Thinking it curious that a child should be alone on the beach at that hour, he decided to check out what was happening.

When he was close enough to speak, he asked the child what he was doing. The child did not look up, but answered while maintaining his frantic pace, "The storm washed all these starfish onto the beach last night. If I don't get them into the ocean before the sun comes up, they will all die."

The man laughed, then said, "I can see what you are doing, but this a long beach and there are thousands of starfish scattered on the shore. Does what you're doing even make a difference?"

The child picked up another starfish, then stood and turned to face the man. "Mister, you may be right, but to *this* starfish, I am the difference!"

The obvious focus of the story is the child. Because of the pending storm, the child anticipates what might happen, then ventures out alone before dawn to investigate. When the problem is confirmed, he voluntarily accepts personal responsibility to fix it, and moves into action. There is no need to be told what to do. There is only the need to act, and there is precious little time to get the job done. The man is only making a hard job even more difficult by missing the moment and wasting his time by being irrelevant to the task, an unfortunately common obstacle for a lifter.

But what does this story tell us about the man? Despite his age, experience, and maturity, he never sees the starfish. Instead, he sees only the "debris" littered along the shore. He has to ask what the child is doing, then ridicules the usefulness of his actions. It never occurs to him to join in the effort because there is nothing in it for him.

He is obviously a leaner because he couldn't lift up a starfish even if there were a $100 bill under it. Nor will he ever get "it" until someone delivers *it* to him, then explains to him what it's all about.

However, we know that since he doesn't see things too clearly, it's very likely that he would not be listening very intently either. In fact the chances are pretty good that he will never understand what makes this child so special.

How often does this happen every day in organizations?

Promote Your Lifters At All Costs, But Disappoint The "Right" People At Every Turn

This story provides a background for the differences between lifters and leaners:

- **Lifters** matter because they elevate the value of their organizations; *leaners* are like matter, because they have weight and take up space.
- **Lifters** are consciously competent, yet constantly striving to improve; *leaners* know what to do but do not exert the effort to consistently do it.
- **Lifters** show others the "art of the possible" by making them feel better about themselves, their jobs and their future opportunities; *leaners* waste time thinking about what the organization owes them for past service.
- **Lifters** "get it" even if they have to go out of their way to find it; *leaners* don't want to be bothered, unless the boss is watching.
- **Lifters** are relevant; *leaners* are redundant.
- **Lifters** seek out muralists; *leaners* are satisfied with monarchs.
- **Lifters** are perpetually "lucky;" *leaners* are chronically unlucky.
- **Lifters** have antlers; *leaners* have horns.

The problem (and challenge) for organizations is that while lifters are supremely motivated they are also quite fragile. How many leaners can they pull along (their bosses as well as their peers) before they get frustrated when their contributions are not sufficiently recognized and rewarded, or realize that they are not getting anywhere or anything fast (except a hernia or a bad back from pulling the dead weight in the process) for their effort?

When the lifters leave the organization, all that is left to be drawn upon for management talent are the leaners who did not pass through the sieve of total incompetency. Over time, the "cult of the monarchic mediocracy" emerges in which the survivors ultimately are measured against the lowest common denominator. The next stage is the organizational death spiral.

The messages are simple: mentor-leaders have learned to protect and promote their lifters at all costs and to disappoint the "right" people at every turn.

So, the next time you see someone walk into a meeting holding onto a "starfish," give them a handshake, a raise and get out of their way. You are probably only slowing them down and holding them back.

You can put the rest of the crew in a rowboat and send them off in a different direction. They can't see where they're headed anyway.

CHAPTER 7

The Questions Are The Same, But The Answers Are Different

"Leading is a privilege earned and not an entitlement owed. Too many leaders and organizations seem to forget...that their authority and ability...to lead is directly related to the willingness of their followers to be led."

Did you ever wonder why graduation is called commencement? You would think that for something that costs so much and takes so long, that the meaning of the actual celebration would have more clarity. For the university administrators, commencement denotes the beginning of life after graduation. Conversely, for many graduates, commencement marks the completion of a milestone and the ending (and often a sad one) of their college experience!

However, as they walk out of the ceremonies, the real question for the graduates is whether they sufficiently understand that their future success is not particularly dependent on what they have learned or currently know. It is far more critical that they have learned how to learn, since they will need to spend the rest of their lives learning, unlearning, and relearning to be successful. Unfortunately, this message is not always clear. The following story illustrates the point.

The Old Professor

An alumnus returns to his college for his 20th reunion. As he walks around the campus, he gets lost among the buildings that have been constructed since his graduation. Finally, he comes across a familiar place and he wanders down the hall. Seeing a light at the end of the corridor, he looks into a classroom and is surprised to recognize his favorite professor, looking much older now, but still working at his desk. The two men begin talking, but the phone rings and the professor steps away. While he's gone, the alumnus sees a copy of a test that had been given that very day. When the professor returns, the alumnus holds up the paper and says, "Do you know that these are the same questions you asked us twenty years ago." The old professor smiles and says, "You're right, the questions are the same, but the answers are different." The alumnus shrugs, "There have been a lot of changes since I was a student here" and soon departs.

The Competition For Relevancy Is Well Underway

This story is interesting because the alumnus seems more taken by the fact that a generation after his graduation, the professor is still giving the same test, than concerned that the world has changed and so have the answers. He sees the obvious changes (new buildings) but has missed the more subtle concept that there is a competition for relevancy underway and he must pay closer attention.

At a basic level everyone understands that things are changing. For example, twenty years ago if the alumnus had stashed a $100 bill under his mattress to be spent at his 20th reunion, it would still have the face value of a hundred bucks, but he is well aware that it will buy fewer beers than in the past. However, at a more elevated level, do "experienced" employees think about, let alone understand, that if their level of learning is twenty years old, "what they know today is not as much as they knew when they learned it"?

Many managers are promoted from within their organizations after years of loyal and dedicated service. While there are definite positives in this kind of career track, it also (perhaps inadvertently) creates a pool of "monarchs-in-waiting" ready to perpetuate traditional practices. Because they are most familiar with historical process, they tend to resist change because they either do not sufficiently understand their need to continually evolve, or they are fearful of their capacity to adapt. Consequently, in the competition for relevancy, they become decreasingly relevant by being increasingly resistive to looking ahead. In essence, while they may claim to have twenty years of experience, what they really have is one year of experience repeated twenty times.

And, what they know is twenty years old.

This is a significant cultural force to be overcome, and it's within this context that many muralistic mentor-leaders must typically function. If their personal energy and philosophical commitment do not exceed the level of organizational resistance, they will get sucked into the cultural quicksand faster than they can realize that they did not have what it took to budge the unmovable object. Sooner or later, despite their best intentions, they will find themselves using the same historical excuses as their employees and become part of a bigger problem.

However, the most forward thinking managers do rise above the hierarchical barriers and organizational legacies to successfully climb their way up the down escalator to become mentor-leaders. They succeed often on only the "brute strength" of their passion and vision. But, just as employees must understand the concept of their ongoing relevance, so must leaders. Even when managers rise to this enlarged leadership role, there are no guarantees they will maintain that position—or stature—in the hearts, minds and actions of their people for longer than the "campaign of the moment."

The Caesar Syndrome

Leadership, after all, creates an ongoing responsibility for leaders to remain relevant due to the strong emotional connections that, at the very least, tacitly and reciprocally bind them to their supporters. Leaders rely on their followers to deliver and support their message just as sports teams depend upon fans to encourage their players. However, followers, like fans, are fickle and cannot be taken for granted. Teams that get rid of favored players, raise ticket prices beyond their perceived value, or compile losing records are constantly reminded how quickly their fan base can erode. The same is true for leaders.

Let's begin with a novel thought. No matter what anyone with a type A ego might think, "The arrogant will not inherit the Earth." Consider Julius Caesar as an example. A brilliant general, visionary, and leader, he was able to enlist his followers to join his cause despite their personal risk to "cross the Rubicon" (the point of no return), to struggle and to win, and then to joyously acclaim him as leader of the Roman Empire. All signs pointed to success. Indeed, "All roads led to Rome."

At some point, however, Caesar "crossed over the line" by allowing himself to become larger than life, disconnected from his cause, and disassociated from his followers. He became more inner focused on being worshipped as a demi-god than on being "follower focused" and serving as their mentor-leader. When his followers realized that his arrogance had broken their emotional contract and corrupted his ability to lead, the end was clear. Caesar was last seen rolling down the stairs of the Senate with a dagger in his back. So much for honorable men, "noblesse oblige," and the thought of a leadership job for life.

Leadership, therefore, is fragile. It is powerful and emotional, but it is not eternal. You would think that Caesar's story, and those of so many other modern day "fallen icons," would serve as continuing reminders that leading is also a privilege earned and not an entitlement owed. Too many leaders and organizations seem to forget to their detriment that their authority and ability (e.g., the privilege) to lead is directly related to the willingness of their followers to be led.

Leading Is Not An Appointment For Life

Therefore, it is just as erroneous to believe that "once a leader always a leader" as it is presumptuous to believe that "once a follower always a follower." Consider the difference between Jimmy Carter and Ronald Reagan. Carter was an unknown populist swept into office in response to the public's distrust of government. He wasn't going to lie; but when it was clear that he was not up to the job, he blamed his failings on the "malaise" of the people and not himself or the government. The people knew better, making him easy prey for Reagan who rallied the country on the theme that America needed a government as good as its people.

When Reagan set the country on a steady course, then stayed with it, he comforted the people with a clear and consistent vision. He established a well-defined mission. Few leaders have ever been better able to communicate and demonstrate "the Feel" of the mentor-leader than Reagan. His ability to tap into the spirit and emotions of people starved for leadership helped him succeed. As a result, when Reagan declared that "America was back and standing tall," they believed him and his popularity soared.

But vision and direction are not everlasting, as even Reagan came to realize. Followers must be continually shown that each new initiative is worthy of their emotion and their involvement (since leaders typically extract a far greater personal commitment than managers). They must also have an ongoing understanding and appreciation for "what's in it for them." The good news is that it is not usually money that starts the ball rolling. Leaders initiate the momentum by helping people "discover" that they are different, that their being different is good, that a different direction is necessary, and then providing the opportunity for their followers to participate with them in making a difference. Without their emotional commitment, there is no sustainable ability to overcome the natural resistance to any new initiative.

The conclusion is simple. The enlarged status of mentor-leader, no matter how well earned, is not an appointment for life. There is a clear line between belief and betrayal, and supporters are ever alert to the difference. Therefore, leaders may have a very short "term in office" if their followers ultimately perceive that their cause was little more than a well-concealed scheme to fulfill personal ambitions, or to serve as a stepping stone from where they can punch their ticket to somewhere else. When trust is given, but promises are not delivered or even reneged upon, widespread commitment is difficult and probably impossible to regain.

But, for muralistic mentor-leaders with "the Feel"; for those who are in concert with the strategy and heartbeat of their business and in tune with the rhythm and pulse of their people, "There ain't no mountain high enough" to scare away their followers. In fact, the higher the mountain and the greater the challenge, the greater their desire to succeed, especially when they must overcome the chronic whining of those who think that the old answers to the old questions are good enough.

There is nothing like that special moment when you stand on top of that hill of personal fulfillment and know that you did it! The bigger the hill, the greater the thrill.

The mere thought of getting there is what gets you out of bed with a rush every morning.

CHAPTER 8

The "Law" Of The Schoolyard

"...Given a choice, most people will opt to succeed. They will surprise you with their resourcefulness and determination. All they need is some help with their technique and a little encouragement from a mentor."

Since leaders are not just born, invented, or educationally transformed, how and where do they get the experience that provides the training, knowledge, and confidence that prepares them to become a mentor-leader? Here's an interesting thought, and it doesn't even cost a dime: take on a real challenge and manage children!

Before dismissing the idea as a time-consuming impossibility, consider that everyone at some point in their life has had to both understand and live within "the law of the schoolyard." As we all learned, this is not an easy place to be. Kids are self-centered and often cruel. They say what's on their mind, no matter how impolite. They are exposed to, and must survive within, the extremes of the mighty and the meek, the popular and the unpopular, the haves and the have nots, and even endure the repulsive apple polishing "Eddie Haskells."

From parents to teachers to coaches and clergy, is there ever another time in our lives as childhood for such constant accountability regarding the rules of conduct? Many of life's permanent lessons are learned within this environment. (When was the last time someone "graded" your performance or gave you a "report card"?)

So, if you want to learn how to lead adults, go back to the common source of their learning and manage children, on the field and in the schoolyard. If you want to know if you've got what it takes, you'll find out fast if you've got "the Feel" by applying your skills with the kids. They are just as direct and difficult as ever and will let you know exactly how you are doing. Even the polite ones are represented by a new generation of increasingly demanding parents, who form a coalition of localized "Home Offices" (but tougher and more personal than their corporate namesakes), who provide either their support, or their opinion, or both.

Every Kid Wants To Catch The Ball

When you think about it, life became competitive the day they put the scoreboard on the Little League field. That's the day that one of life's three great lies, "It's not whether you win or lose, but how you play the game," was exposed. The newspapers are filled with stories of misguided parental behavior related to winning. However, contrary to what some overly exuberant parents might think, the only thing of lasting value is the learning that occurs in the practices and during the games that endures long after the scores are forgotten.

For instance, line a team of first-year little leaguers against a backstop and toss the ball to each kid. Although every youngster wants to catch it, many will fail. Some managers will think that this exercise provides sufficient training, and after the quickest of ability assessments, relegate (banish?) the lesser skilled players to the outfield, where they are not likely to improve, and from where they are unlikely to escape.

Fortunately, other managers understand the urgent need and eager desire of every kid to make the play and hear the encouraging words, "nice catch" when they succeed, or even "nice try" when they do not. They create a nonthreatening learning environment in which the youngsters can overcome their fears and skill deficits. As their confidence improves, their skills develop and the kids are able to learn, progress, and have more fun in the process. Managers with this kind of attitude become magnets for parents. They have "the Feel" of the larger picture. Parents want their kids to be on their team, and they will volunteer to pick up the bats and balls, and even buy the ice cream when the practices are over. These managers are the volunteer muralists-in-training.

Like It Or Not, All Eyes Are On The Manager

However, what happens when the manager is constantly screaming at the players, does not work with them sufficiently enough to increase their skill levels, or makes the experience unenjoyable? Sadly, the answer is metaphorical to adult life because there are monarchs of the schoolyard as well. Children, like adults, either develop coping skills because they love the game (and learn to tune the manager out) or become so fearful of the manager's wrath from dropping the ball or striking out that their learning stops, their interest in the game fades, and they create scenes at home that take out their failings and hurt feelings on the ones who love them the most. Ultimately they either quit, or their parents demand that they be placed on another team, before denouncing the manager to any other parent who will listen.

The lesson is this: the manager matters! Whatever the level of play, or wherever management is being practiced, people watch and evaluate the manager. This is what makes managing children so valuable an opportunity to develop "the Feel." Even where managing is voluntary, there is an expectation by someone in "authority" (e.g., the "Home Office") that the manager will do a good job or face the consequences. This does not necessarily mean winning, and it definitely does not mean hormonally competing with other managers to the detriment of the children.

The good news is that what most parents want is for their kids to play, to learn, and to have fun. This means you need to become organized, set up practices that help them improve, make certain that everyone gets in the game, build up their self esteem and earn the confidence of their "home office" that you have the bigger picture in clear view.

These are standard elements of managing. If the kids tell their parents that they like their manager and run uncomplainingly to practice, you are probably on the right track.

Of course, for a minority of parents, winning every game is crucial. Like problem customers, they create stressful challenges and emotion which the manager must learn how to anticipate, address, endure, and overcome. Where else can you get such a valuable experience that can be instantly reapplied to your job?

You Have To Get Your Players In The Game

What happens when the coach has set the wrong priorities? My son played on a Pop Warner football team when he was ten years old. The weight limit was 90 pounds, so all the kids were quite small. One player in particular was among the smallest and least aggressive. Nevertheless, he was on the field every day, practicing with his friends but taking much more of a beating than he gave out. He never complained to the coach, but on Sundays when he was all dressed up and his parents were in the stands, he just sat on the bench. This embarrassed him in front of his friends and made him miserable at home with his parents. The father called the coach and politely asked if he would put his son into the game so that he would feel better about the experience. The coach said he would take it into consideration.

What the coach really believed was that the boy was not a good player and the team's chances of winning were reduced when he played. However, by not letting him play, the coach had made at least three big mistakes:

- He had lost sight of his primary objectives and responsibilities.
- If the player was actually better than the coach believed, he would have "gained" a player and made the team stronger.
- Until the player got into the game, the parents were entitled to think that their kid was being denied the opportunity to be a potential all star by an arrogant coach who wouldn't give him a chance.

When the parents angrily confronted the coach during the next game and demanded that their son be put into the action, a loud scene on the sidelines ensued in clear view of every parent and player. The coach loudly referenced the parents with unflattering names, and told them in no uncertain terms that the team was his, and that only the best players would get on the field. Right then and there, the parents removed the shirt from their child, left his helmet at the coach's feet and stormed off. The players on the field were so upset at what was happening to their friend that they stopped playing. The team lost the game.

The coach was not on the sidelines the following week. He blamed the parents, but it was quite clear that he had no "Feel" for coaching kids and even less hope that he could lead adults. Sadly, it was too late for the youngster, who never played organized sports again.

The lesson here is simple. Once you spend the time training your team, you have the responsibility to get your players into the game to see what they can do! You must provide an equal opportunity for them to succeed or fail. However, it's up to them to take your training and apply it when it counts. They will usually surprise you with their desire to succeed. But if you keep them on the sidelines, neither you nor they will ever know what they are capable of adding to your organization.

The Gymnast

My daughter was a gymnast. I would sit in the stands for hours watching the coach teach new moves to the team. While all the girls were eager to try anything new in the floor exercise, the balance beam was another matter altogether. As if the beam was not narrow enough, the three "Fs" (fear, falling, and failure) were additional obstacles to be overcome.

The coach knew that most of the gymnasts were determined to compete to their best level, so he was very patient and supportive with them as he put together their beam routines. He never yelled, in fact, the calm of his voice tended to provide them with reassurance, despite the personal risks inherent on this apparatus. He did not ask them to do anything of which they were not capable; but when they could successfully perform a new maneuver twice in practice, it was in the routine.

One night, in front of the largest crowd of the season, a middle-of-the-lineup gymnast on a bottom-of-the-standings team was ready to perform her most advanced move for the first time. The gym was silent as she stood on the beam ready to make the attempt. Unfortunately, when she stepped into her move she missed her mark and she began to roll off the beam. Instinctively, she caught her arm on the bar as she fell, then quickly swung her legs around so she was left hanging upside down, her back suspended between the floor and the beam, and her arms and legs straddled above.

There was a burst of nervous laughter from the stands at this unusual sight, but there was nothing funny about what happened next. The laughter turned into an eerie silence as everyone watched her engage in an incredible personal struggle. With her coach gently urging her on, the gymnast literally, and without even the slightest pretext of grace, willed herself back onto the beam. You can imagine the scene, and perhaps even "hear" her grunting as she finally got her leg over the bar and pulled herself up. Then with unbelievable determination and emotion, she re-attempted the same maneuver and succeeded. When she landed her dismount, the crowd went wild and her teammates embraced her as though she had won a gold medal. What a moment! What a life-changing confidence booster.

The lesson here is that given a choice, most people will opt to succeed. They will surprise you with their resourcefulness and determination. All they need is some help with their technique and a little encouragement from a mentor whose management style and support matter even more than they probably understand.

Therefore, a leader with a steady hand and guiding influence can enhance the likelihood of personal growth by creating an environment that encourages their people to be "comfortably uncomfortable" as they stretch their skills to new limits, despite the personal risk. The coach could not guarantee that the gymnast would not fail, but his leadership style convinced her that she would not reach the next level of her potential until she pictured herself succeeding and dared to make her move. Her life will always be different as a result of him. This is what muralistic mentor-leaders do—they make a difference.

Setting The Strategy—Can Three Beat Five?

A volunteer coach had a basketball team of junior high school boys. While they all enjoyed the game, with the exception of three players their enthusiasm exceeded their level of skill. After three games they had three lopsided losses and a low team morale. A long season seemed likely.

The coach's choices were simple—accept the team for what it was (after all, it was only a game) or find a way to better utilize his team's talent to win. He decided to find a way in which three good players could defeat teams with five good players. The coach needed a strategy.

What he ultimately realized was that he needed to better optimize the capabilities of his team's "human assets" by assigning the most appropriate roles and responsibilities that best fit each player. When he had developed his plan, the coach positioned his three most skilled players on one side of the court. Another player was placed on the opposite side and given the responsibility of being the team's fiercest rebounder. The fifth player was placed at the top of the circle and tasked with the role of ace defender and ball stealer.

They repeatedly practiced plays which allowed the team to match its three best players against three players from the other team. By narrowing the court to keep at least two defenders away from the action around the ball, the talent equation shifted, and often favored his team due to their strategy (focused practice, improved play execution, and more defined roles and responsibilities).

The team's designated role players became quickly motivated by their success in their "key" responsibilities. The rebounders were praised for every ball they caught, and the defenders were cheered for every steal they made. As the team began winning, their confidence increased and they even began scoring as well. Before long there were more than three "good" players and the team lost only one more game the rest of the season.

Similarly, most businesses have more demands than top people to handle them. They also have more issues to handle and deadlines to manage than time to complete them. When this happens, should managers just throw up their hands, declare defeat and go home? Like the coach, leaders need to prioritize their business issues, evaluate their strategic assets, and draw the play on the "chalk board" for everyone to see what they must do (e.g., muralize). Top performers must be challenged to deliver greater results on the highest priorities, and less experienced performers made more comfortably uncomfortable by being stretched to take on issues of increasing significance.

By placing employees in situations where they are appropriately challenged, coached, and cheered, they will learn, progress and succeed. They will even have fun as they contribute to the team's success. It happens every day. All they need is a chance, and the confidence from knowing that there is somebody on their side and in their corner.

Ask managers how they can do more with less. Many will just shake their heads and tell you it cannot be done. But, "upsets" happen because good coaches with a better conceived strategy for effectively prioritizing their objectives, and using their assets to efficiently attack their opposition, make them happen all the time. In other words, upsets seldom just happen by luck. So, before accepting the response from managers that "three can't beat five," send them to strategy school working with the kids.

The Boy And The Mums

A man moved into a new house. He brought a patch of garden mums from his old home with him (a gift from his grandmother many years earlier) and began planting them in his new yard. His neighbor's seven-year-old son saw him digging, so he grabbed his little shovel and asked if he could help. When his mother saw this, she suggested that her son could find something else to do if he was being a bother. The man insisted that he was a big help. Before they finished, he gave the boy a clump of mums and asked if he could help him plant them in his yard. For the rest of the summer, the boy watered the mums in both yards. Sure enough, there were beautiful flowers in the fall.

This continued for several years. They divided the plants together in the spring, watered them in the summer, and enjoyed the flowers in the fall. But the man moved during the deep freeze of January when the mums were buried under a foot of snow. In the spring, the boy's parents also moved. But as his family made its way to their new address, the boy made them stop at their former neighbor's new house—so he could personally deliver half the mums he had dug up from his yard to replant at his new home.

Many years later, the much older man still cannot look at the blooms on those plants in the fall without seeing the face of that little boy.

The lesson here is clear. Not only can managers lead children, managers also can learn from children. The same is true with adults on the job. Monarchs believe that knowledge is power and withhold information to exert personal control. However, this story reveals that by investing time and energy, and sharing knowledge with either a child or their colleagues, muralists ultimately receive far more in return than they originally give.

Inspiration And Perspiration

The common theme of all of these stories is that there is a "law of the schoolyard" that everyone knows and understands. Adults constantly remember and reference their childhood stories throughout their lives. It's how we learned right and wrong behaviors when we were learning how to act within our various "environments." Indeed, most adults go through their lives unwittingly attempting to reapply these laws, although not nearly as efficiently, effectively, directly, or honestly as they did when they were kids.

- Monarchs, like the football coach, attempt to bypass these "laws" with a more disciplined, demeaning, and despotic set of rules. This can be effective for a while, but sooner or later there will be an uprising against their abuse of authority, resulting in failure. Perhaps monarchs should hang a picture of Caesar on their wall as a reminder of failed arrogance.
- Muralists, like the gymnastics coach, work patiently with their athletes to help them overcome their fears by providing training within a safe environment and by helping them to visualize their success in real life. Their lessons are deeper and more positively life-changing because they focus on optimizing the skill level of each athlete, not forcing the athlete to fit into a predetermined routine.
- Because life is not always fair, and resources seldom plentiful enough, managers must develop effective and creative strategies to be successful. How better to learn this skill than by developing strategic game plans that emphasize the skills and values of all their assets, or learning how to adjust to unanticipated events on the fly during the fast-paced action of a basketball or soccer game, or other activity?

It is likely that managing children for even just one year has more practical impact, longer lasting value, and greater business relevancy than a management degree. Mentor-leaders learn and understand that when they supply the inspiration, their followers (adults or children) will provide the perspiration. All you have to do is say, "nice catch" when they make it, and "nice try" when they don't. Given an opportunity to succeed or fail, they will almost always choose to succeed. They are typically not afraid of putting in the time, effort, energy, or emotion especially when it is appreciated and reciprocated.

Therefore, working with children and understanding how they behave provides not only a service to the community, but also significant training and insight ("the Feel") for adult behavior.

The price is right—so do it. You'll never be the same again. You'll be better! Along the way, you will receive an infusion of energy and a jolt of enthusiasm from the idealistic passion of the kids.

Be prepared. One day, someone will unexpectedly deliver a mum to your door and remind you of a life lesson that you had taught them—a "keeper" that you had long forgotten, but that they had remembered and are ready to pass back to you. You'll be overwhelmed by the experience.

That's when you really begin to understand what you have achieved and the difference that you have made.

It will even help you shed some of your adult cynicism.

CHAPTER 9

Put Your Name On The Door

"When you turn on the lights and greet your people, remember that you are the one who is expected to make the first move and behave like a leader. It's not about somebody else, it's about you. Your people will initially be patient, but their patience is not eternal. If you don't act quickly, the moment will be lost and the job will never be yours."

When does "your" job truly become yours?

The question may be more complex and deserve more thought than you may think, which is why you need to know about the story of Paul and Betsy.

A manager received a promotion and relocated with his family to a new city. After a few weeks of house hunting, the realtor advised them of their stroke of good luck. Paul and Betsy, a very popular couple in the area, were unexpectedly moving and their home had just been listed for sale. The realtor was certain that this was the right home for them because it was a beautiful house in a lovely neighborhood and in a great location. Sure enough, they bought it. In three years the couple moved to another city. A short while later the manager bumped into a former neighbor at the airport and asked what was new in the neighborhood. "Nothing much, really," he said, "except somebody new moved into Paul and Betsy's house."

Occupancy Does Not Mean Ownership

Did that manager ever really "own" that house? Obviously not! Residency does not necessarily equal ownership within the context of a neighborhood. The same is true in organizations. Many managers "reside

49

in," yet never own their jobs. They move into a new assignment and occupy their predecessor's former office, but they fail to understand or execute the key component of the transition—the act of putting their name on the door.

There is a limited window of opportunity to establish ownership, yet despite every chance to successfully assimilate into, then lead their new operations to improved levels of performance, too few managers make a name for themselves.

This can not only be damaging to the new manager, it can be even more devastating to the person who put them into the job. Higher level managers are looking for a quick, positive validation of their decisions. Their degree of impatience intensifies if the selection process had many good applicants or if a qualified local favorite was bypassed for the position.

Whoever gets the job, there are expectations to be achieved, and hopefully exceeded, but, the timetable is not eternal. For instance, in addition to the basic job requirements, the boss might specifically expect a deviation from the prior status quo, or demonstrably increased energy and contagious enthusiasm, or new direction and more focused initiatives, or improved levels of communications and more visible leadership from their newly appointed managers. However, if there are no signs of a productive heartbeat in a reasonable time, the writing is on the wall before their name is etched on the door.

In the end, the important thing to remember is that every job is about its incumbent. Therefore, for better or for worse, every job you hold is about you, and derivatively (as the manager) your entire organization. In this sense, Louis XVI had it right when he declared, "L'etat c'est moi." Unfortunately for him, when the people ran out of food, they also ran out of patience and Louie's head ran out of shoulder space.

While the HR culture today is less "cutting edge," ineffective leaders are being eliminated with increasing speed. The reason is clear. Organizations do take on the personality of their leader. When the leader begins to smell, their odor ultimately permeates through their organization until everything and everyone else connected to it also begins to stink—even if the perceptions are unfair (which they usually are). Since the people are typically better than their "leaders," the fix is obvious. The good news is that the reverse situation is equally true—a fact well known by muralists!

The Unspoken Question—
Why Did You Get The Job?

Not only is validating the boss' choice a challenge to be overcome, but fitting in with your peers is another big hurdle. Peers anxiously await a demonstration of what the new manager next door can do and why they got the job. They quietly, but nervously, watch and wonder if this appointment will raise the competitive level of their own expected performance, re-order their position in the "pecking order," change the social dynamic of the office, or just stick them with another needy newcomer that they are expected to train before they become useful or productive.

If the new manager does not have the stuff, or chooses to take information but share none in exchange, or behaves like a self-centered "solo lobo," the organizational resistance will move quickly into action, and the manager's name will probably be on the corporate obituary page long before it's on the door.

Subordinates are also well aware of what is (or, more often, what is not) happening. In their mind "that office," and all that goes along with it, must be earned. New managers become rapidly irrelevant when they fail to quickly substantiate or clearly demonstrate the reasons why they were appointed, especially when their competencies do not meet those of their predecessor's or they set a course in a different direction. After their newness fades, the inevitable comparisons begin and people begin to refer to "their" position as their predecessor's old job. By the time the whispers turn into words that are freely spoken, the drums are beating signifying that it is only a matter of time before the next new manager arrives.

Why New Managers Fail

Why do so many managers fail long before their names are on their doors?

- They fail when they do not articulate a coherent philosophy to their employees, or fail to stick with one.
- They fail when they need to credentialize themselves, but cannot pass the credibility test.
- They fail when they act as though they do not understand their place or role in the larger organization, leaving their subordinates derivatively adrift and uncomfortably uncertain of their roles.
- They fail when they believe that employees will passively accept their arrogance as a higher life form of intelligence.
- They fail when they do not think strategically, or develop the creative skills of the muralist, or take charge of their new position.
- They fail when they delegate everything, but accept accountability for nothing.
- They fail when they take credit even when the praise belongs to someone else.
- They fail when they cannot look you in the eye and shake your hand at the same time.

- They fail when employees know more about them than they know about their employees.
- They fail when they engage in too much ass covering and not enough trust creation.
- They fail when they neither "own" the passion of their work force, nor earn their trust.
- They fail when they occupy an office whose door is constantly closed, and from which they seldom emerge.
- And, in the end, they fail when they neither dare to be different nor make a difference.

It's pretty basic — a leader needs followers, and the followers need to be convinced that the leader is capable and trustworthy of guiding them in the right direction. The leaders who provide a consistent philosophy, demonstrate "the Feel", and give their employees the confidence to believe in them and their future do not need to put their name on their door as proof of ownership. Their people will do it for them, and defend it when they are not there.

Conversely, managers who provide little hope for improvement and even less inspiration, who do not tap into the passion and energy of their employees, and who consequently fail to produce to their level of expectations, could have a neon nameplate on the door and still not own their jobs. They become trivia answers the next time employees sit around the water cooler venting about their managers.

A Manager Discovered, A Manager Lost

As a result, too many managers get lost at the very time they have been seemingly "discovered." By not definitively putting their name on their door, they plod along as corporate caretakers, thinking that strategy is someone else's job, and that leading is something that their boss does as badly to them as they do to everyone else. Their careers move along a continuum that quickly runs its course from conscious competence to conscious complacency. At some point they become so mired in their comfort zone that they begin concentrating more on retirement, or quitting, than their business or the people who are dependent on them for guidance and leadership. They are in the "land of the living dead" but either do not know it or no longer care.

If you don't believe that this is true, consider the number of retirement or farewell luncheons you have attended, and ask yourself what was said about the honorees as they were walking out the door. They were probably referenced as fine ladies and gentlemen; people you could go to for advice with trust and confidence. Perhaps that's the most that can be expected. It's as though a colorless existence is viewed as a good thing—that most people, including managers, are valued for faithfully obeying throughout their careers and keeping their heads down and mouths closed (except when meeting in groups to whine about their bosses). How monarchically manipulative!

How many times have you heard that the departing person was a leader, expressed in passionate terms and in a factual context that everyone could understand and appreciate because they knew it is was true? How often are private tears quietly wept by those who benefited most from their mentoring? Sadly, not too frequently. This can only happen for the few who choose to make it happen by being relevant, by taking the risk while creating the trust, by cultivating and captivating their supporters, including their peers, by developing "the Feel," by daring to be different and by ascending to the position of mentor-leader.

Think about this for a moment. How would you feel if your gravestone proclaimed as your greatest career achievement, "Here lies John or Jane, a reliable person and decent manager who maintained perfect attendance for every day of their life, except the last?"

Compare this to Paul and Betsy, the popular couple in their neighborhood whose names remained on the door long after they had left the building.

Therefore, if you want to lead and begin earning your "points," it all begins with a simple, though profound, act—putting your name on your door.

When you turn on the lights and greet your people, remember that you are the one who is expected to make the first move and behave like a leader. It's not about somebody else, it's about you. Your people will initially be patient, but their patience is not eternal. If you don't act quickly, the moment will be lost and the job will never be yours.

So, practice what you intend to say and do in the first minute, during the first hour, on your first day, and at your first meeting on your new job—and make it count! How you behave will be forgotten by you long before it's forgotten by them.

It's up to you.

CHAPTER 10

Out Of The Box Thinking ...And Other Myths

"The very use of the words, 'out of the box' suggests that we have all been categorically placed in a preordained 'box' in which we will remain until we have the knowledge or ability to escape...You will ultimately spend eternity in a box. Why, then, would you allow yourself to be involuntarily placed into one while you are alive and kicking and have controllable options?"

Do you find yourself feeling a little perplexed or even angry when your manager tells you that "your problem" is that you don't "think out of the box," or complains about your inability to "color outside the lines," as if these are the cultural norms, or part of your job description? This is another remnant of the leadership paradox. Most managers use control as a power tool and have a distaste for those daring to stray too far off the ranch. Yet at some point, typically at review time, you hear the words "doesn't think out of the box" and your name in the same sentence, and you can't believe your ears.

Is Everyone Assigned To A Box Until They Escape?

The very use of the words, "out of the box," suggests that we have all been categorically placed in a preordained "box" in which we will remain until we have the knowledge or ability to escape. For those who aspire to the position of mentor-leader, that moment cannot come soon enough.

Think about it this way, you will ultimately spend eternity in a box. Why, then, would you allow yourself to be involuntarily placed into one while you are alive and kicking and have controllable options?

But this raises another point. Do managers really want their employees to be different, even when they are creatively (and productively) deviating from established standards to achieve a better result? Or is this merely rhetoric and of value only when they have no other earthly idea of what to do, or they are being pressed for a solution by their boss?

Due to their obedient, political, and fear-ridden tendencies, monarchs will do virtually anything to get their bosses what they think they need, including making a temporary deviation from the rules, if that's what's required to get positive recognition. This might provide short-term hope to their employees that things are changing. However, as soon as the "all clear" sounds and the fire drill is over, most everything reverts to normal, unless the big boss likes the creative solution (which then becomes the new and blessed norm), or the monarch has taken credit for the solution without appropriate acknowledgment of their subordinates who actually did the work (which assures the manager's place in infamy and updated resumes by everyone else).

But telling someone to prepare an "out of the box" solution is difficult under most circumstances. Employees are typically not comfortable with the concepts of "no boundaries" and "blue sky" thinking. They are more comfortable wearing their uniform and marching in the parade. Why do you think people constantly complain when they feel as though they are left "out on a limb" without sufficient direction and even less support? They feel more vulnerable than powerful out there. It's not as though there is an "out of the box" drawer in everyone's mind overflowing with creative solutions eagerly awaiting their debut. For the most part, employees know how to identify, even create, problems far more easily than they can offer feasible fixes, especially when the cure is uncomfortable or inconvenient for them.

Think Evolution, *Not* Revolution

How do muralists do it? How are these leaders able to help their employees shed the historical burden of conventional thinking and transform them into "out of the box" thinkers?

The answer is different from what you may think.

Despite what might be said, there is little value in proposed solutions that are so far out of the norm that they are quickly dismissed for being too far out of the question. When the solutions are too vague or too revolutionary, the natural organizational defenses against change rise up in resistance. Therefore, muralists effectively show their teams how to win by thinking, working, and acting *inside* the box and by coloring within the lines in order to produce *evolutionary* solutions.

This is different from the follow-the-rules and do what you're told philosophy of monarchs because it is a far more rational and organizationally holistic. The process begins with an analysis and understanding of the established strategy and business issues. Options are developed and decisions are made within these contexts. In the end, muralists succeed because they work within the operating framework of the organization to create workable solutions by elevating expectations and raising performance to higher levels. They just take a different path to get there.

Along the way, muralists create an "elite status" within their teams that consistently shows, and measurably proves that as far as the operational plan is concerned, they not only "get it," but they can deliver it, and fast. However, none of this has significant value until they can persuasively sell their concepts and solutions within the organization and get their plan in motion. Execution and delivery are the keys. An "out of the box plan" that cannot be operationally implemented because it has little or no support creates as much organizational noise as the latest "outside the lines" idea that falls unheard in an empty conference room. Both are DOA, if not sooner.

The following are two developmental techniques that mentor-leaders can use to coach their teams how to become muralists-in-training by creating "out of the box" solutions, while coloring within the lines. The first can best be described as the "back of the maze" philosophy-in-action; the latter is a new way of looking at a common and inexpensive pastime that can be used to concurrently develop teamwork, vision, and deductive thinking.

Both, not so coincidentally, are played within the physical confines of "the box"!

Why So Many Managers Have Flat Heads

Did you ever wonder why so many managers have flat heads? Imagine that all projects, problems, or business issues appear in the form of mazes with the "start" at the top and the "finish" at the bottom. In their best monarch-like tradition, most managers follow the "rules" and begin at the start by rowing their way down every path (moving forward while looking backward), project statement in one hand and rule book in the other, banging the backs of their heads into every blind alley of the maze along the way.

If their stamina is strong enough and their team does not mutiny before they make it (neither a certainty by any measure), they will ultimately arrive at the exit, declare victory, and take credit for their team's courage and perseverance. It's as though they enjoy banging their heads against the walls because it makes them feel all the better when they stop. What they do not mention is the wasted time, effort, and energy expended just to achieve the minimum requirement—to escape from the maze—whatever the cost or the casualty count.

The Rorschach On The Wall

Conversely, muralists begin the process by assembling their teams to review the project and scope it within the context of the organizational strategy. The first objective is the exploration and agreement of "what it will look like" when they have completed the project. Everyone participates in a "free think" forum, a form of a "tossing ideas against the wall to see what sticks" exercise (e.g., "muralizing"). The only "rule" is that all members must contribute their ideas to ensure that everyone is in the game and that one person does not provide all of the "best" thinking (or the most noise).

While many of the ideas will slide off the wall, what sticks is mutually owned and becomes the focus of the ongoing dialogue. The evolution of ideas continues until everyone can "see" what *it* will look like when the project is done.

As a result, when the "Rorschach on the wall" finally does reveal its shape, the deliverable objective is typically clearer to see and richer in content due to the enthusiastic and untethered participation of the team members, not to mention the additive effects from their diversity of experience. It also helps everyone envision the final product and the process to get there.

In contrast to monarchs, therefore, the entry point for muralists is the "back of the maze." Working backwards from the envisioned end result and kayaking towards the start, the team more easily identifies what needs to be done, and foresees what obstacles must be avoided to quickly reach their objectives. This saves time, energy, and "flat heading," which creates a highly motivated team that works quickly and efficiently to deliver a better result.

The Puzzle

Here's a second exercise that was born from working with my daughter when she was in college. Despite her intelligence, I was surprised that she would regularly call each night with questions that she should probably have been able to answer for herself with a little more thought. Concerned by her apparent lack of self-confidence and troubling need to have her parents figure out her problems, I sent her a 1,000 piece jigsaw puzzle—without the box—as a Valentine's Day gift.

The note in my card was clear, simple, and loving. When she and her Harvard roommates could call and correctly identify the picture I would take them all to a restaurant of their choice as long as they could provide the following details over our dinner:

• how they organized their assembly process without the picture on the box as a frame of reference,
• the number of pieces *not* in the puzzle when they made their call, and
• what they had learned in the process.

What a hit! Within a few days I got the call. By quickly building their borders, then working inside the framework of the puzzle, they grouped similar pieces by colors and shapes, then identified and worked with the puzzle's visual clues. Each roommate had assigned tasks, but they communicated openly while completing them. Their efforts quickly paid off when the puzzle's image suddenly emerged allowing them to complete their challenge with just over 50% of the pieces in place. Their call was as enthusiastic as Archimedes' "Eureka" (but fortunately not as demonstrative).

What they learned was that by working together to reach their objective, they were more quickly able to organize their tasks and communicate freely to achieve their goal, even without all of the information on the board. In fact, they intuitively learned the value (a good dinner) of making a good, but informed, decision quickly versus waiting to make a more certain call after a more exhaustive examination of the data (more puzzle pieces) that would have added little to their decision, but delayed it considerably.

My daughter also learned that she could make more of her decisions without 100% of the facts, or the questionable assistance of her parents.

I subsequently have used this "game" as a training exercise with adults. The reaction and results have been the same "when they get it." The exercise becomes the lasting metaphor for working out issues in daily operations.

Like the lesson of the lily pads, nobody forgets the principles of the puzzle game!

CHAPTER **11**

The Same Place We Crashed Last Year

"...when business traditions are passed down...it doesn't take long before the newer employees don't know or cannot understand why they began in the first place."

One question that has to be going through your mind by now is that if muralistic mentor-leader is the desired state for managers, why don't they all just become one? If only it were as easy as making the preferred selection from a menu of management styles. However, (but unfortunately) most managers have already "learned how to manage" from their current and prior experiences while being managed as employees themselves. Since most employees can recall few, if any, good leaders from among their past managers, this is not positive news. Consider the consequences from the following story.

The Caribou Story

A general manager and two subordinates chartered a plane to go caribou hunting in a northern wilderness two hundred miles away. As they landed in a clearing the pilot confirmed when he would return and reminded them that the plane's capacity could carry the three hunters and one caribou. Several days later the pilot returned but was quickly incensed by the sight of three caribou waiting in the clearing. He made no secret of his displeasure even after the general manager offered him $500 to load the animals onto the plane. Angered by the delay, one of the subordinates complained, "What's your problem? Last year you took our money and thought nothing of it." The pilot, quickly answered, "Last year you only had two caribou." After a quick huddle, the managers offered $1,000 to load all three. The pilot agreed and pocketed the cash. They quickly loaded the caribou on board and the plane took off. But, just when it had climbed above the tree line, the plane fell like a rock and crashed into the woods. After a few moments the general manager yelled out, "Does anybody know where we are?" From across the forest the pilot bellowed back, "The same place we crashed last year!"

What is the likelihood that the same outcome will be repeated (again) next year?

The Word Is "Celebrate"

This story is sadly reflective of many hierarchical organizations that perpetuate the same tired old myths and questionable management practices year after year. One generation of managers is replaced by the next, but there is little or no change in the process because their knowledge and experiences have been the same. They have all been marching to the same beat along the same route for years. Therefore, when a drum major retires, their successor already knows the directions to that same dead end road by heart and is applauded for not "missing a beat." After all, there's nothing like a smooth transition to ensure traditional thinking.

However, when business traditions are passed down from one business generation to the next, it doesn't take long before the newer employees don't know or cannot understand why they began in the first place. Nevertheless, the remaining old-timers speak reverently of past managers as though they were legends, defying anyone to change the sacraments of their wisdom. This behavior certainly creates intergenerational linkage, but the net effect can be dysfunctional, if not incalculably harmful. For instance:

Quality Assurance?

A managing monk transfers into a new monastery and finds that the monks are hand scripting their books from the latest copy and not the original version. He points out that if an error was made in transcription, the subsequent copies would be similarly flawed for eternity. When he tries to change the process he meets organizational resistance because the procedure in that monastery had been in place for generations.

To prove his point, he announces that he is going to conduct a quality assurance review of the latest copy by comparing it to the original stored in the cellar. The monks are outraged, but when he does not return in a few hours, one of the more compassionate monks becomes concerned and goes looking for him.

He finds him weeping uncontrollably in the corner of the cellar. "What's wrong?" he asks. The managing monk can hardly speak, but after a few moments he looks up and sighs, "The word is celebrate."

This can happen in families just as easily, which is probably why it is so generally tolerated at work. While many family traditions are warm and loving, some perpetuate for generations through guilt and fear. Woe to the free-spirited family members ("black sheep") who attempt to exercise too much control over their lives or pay disrespect to their elders by deviating from time-honored customs. The tendency, therefore, is to get into mental lockstep with the past because it's easier, safer, less emotional, and besides, who wants to mess with the matriarch and her traditions?

The good news is that times change, and "customs" can and should be changed along with them, by those with the curiosity to learn and the need to understand why they began in the first place, and the courage to decide if they are still relevant.

That's The Way My Mother Did It

Examples of dysfunctional traditions abound, like the newlywed who cooked a leg of lamb for her first post-wedding dinner. Her husband loved the meal but was curious as to why she had used a hacksaw to cut the hind quarter of the meat and cooked the smaller piece alongside the rest of the leg. He was told that was the way her mother did it.

A few months later his mother-in-law cooked a lamb dinner using the same process. When he asked why she had hacksawed the hind quarter, she said that her mother had always done it that way.

By good fortune, the grandmother was still alive and at the next holiday she also cooked a lamb dinner, but without a hacksaw in sight. When the young husband told her the story and asked the obvious question, the grandmother laughed and told him that in the old days, when families were large and ovens were small, she had to cut the lamb into pieces to get it all into a pan that would fit in the oven. However, she hadn't done that for over twenty years since she had bought a larger oven.

And yet, her "tradition" continued for two subsequent generations and would be continuing today had the grandmother not been alive to tell the rest of the story (but only after someone new to the process was curious enough to ask). How many retirees would laugh if they knew that they still held the secrets to their company's legacies? What if they did not think that those "sacred" procedures were so great even in their best day?

Up The Down Escalator

How do leaders emerge from within such constraining environments? They must break down the barriers of resistance with persistent energy, enthusiasm, and a philosophy relevant to the changing times and current challenges.

Compare the cultural challenges of the twelve point buck with those of a leader. Neither achieves their status overnight, nor without significant experience and consistent success. To earn its "points," the buck must successfully adapt to the extremes of its "business" environment (winters, drought, food supply). It must be stronger than its internal competitors (other bucks) to maintain its status and relevance within its "organization," while also being smarter than its external competition (predators and hunters) to survive.

Leaders face similar (though less harsh) challenges. When employees ask "What's in it for them," leaders earn their points by standing taller than the tallest, clearly defining their vision and communicating why their objectives, their sense of direction, and their leadership are worthy of their employees' confidence. This is the essence of muralizing. The muralist paints a mental picture in colors that are so clear and bold that employees can "see" the vision and actually picture themselves being successful within it, yet also includes the subtle tones that help them understand why the vision is important to the organization and worthy of their involvement.

To do this, the mentor-leader must know, understand, and have the feel of the pulse of the people and the heartbeat of the business. But knowing and doing are two different things. Anyone who has ever taken a shower or gone for a walk has had ideas. The key is in the doing, the actual execution.

An important difference between managers and leaders is that leaders make their ideas happen. To be successful, they must not only personally initiate the necessity for change, but also clearly, consistently, and continually communicate the urgent need for change. They must take personal responsibility for making it happen. Without the leader's sweat equity and personal identification with the effort, the initiative will fail due to a lack of followers and from the natural resistance to change steeped within the organization's culture.

In many ways muralistic leaders' ability to create change is the equivalent of pulling their organization forward while running up a down escalator. It's hard work. Resistant monarchs stand at the top of the moving stairs, increasing the speed to retard their progress and slowing them down with calls for conformity, adherence to traditions, and protection of the organization's sacred cows as they make their ascent.

The employees are spectators to the event, watching from the "virtual" grandstand of the arena. Some doubters want the up-and-coming leaders to fail because they are comfortable where they are and do not want the organization to change. The more daring will even actively attempt to undermine the new plan and subvert the effort. Their active resistance will be supplemented by the less confident, passive aggressors who hide in the shadows and either drag their heels in defiance or talk about being "the devil's advocate" and other nonsense.

However, others watch and wait in silent admiration, wishing and hoping that these different leaders possess the skill, nerve, and persistence to endure the struggle and liberate them.

It's not an easy road, but that's why they call it leading, and that's why too few can do it. When you make it to the top with your brains intact and your feet still under you, don't be surprised to find yourself so overwhelmed with emotion from the sense of accomplishment that you actually weep when you think nobody is looking. Believe it or not, it's a great feeling.

While leading presents interesting and often unique challenges, if you have the endurance and the heart to make it, you will find that you will never be alone. When leaders lead, their people will follow. The truest believers will be there for you at every step along the route, but more followers will be awaiting your arrival at the finish line. One will give you a towel, and another will buy you a drink. However, all of them will give you their admiration and respect.

At some point, when nobody is around and "the coast is clear," someone will shake your hand, look you in the eye, and tell you that "You're different." When you get back to your office, your name will be on the door. Your life will never be the same again, and you will never look back.

Too few managers ever experience that thrill. If they did, there would doubtless be more leaders.

What all this means is that next year when those managers offer the pilot $5,000 to load the caribou onto the plane, they will still crash, and wonder why. They will never know even though the answer is obvious. Arrogance is not to be confused with leading, and, leading is not to be confused with doing what everybody else is doing.

Leaders seldom have to say that they're different. Anyone who is anybody already knows it.

CHAPTER 12

Does Everybody Really Love A Parade?

"... it all begins at the top. Employees are very impressed by leaders who roll up their sleeves, know their business, remember their names, understand their problems, speak empathetically and can explain their vision, objectives and problems openly and plainly—and with an occasional sense of humor."

Long before they hear the drums in the distance or feel the excitement from the marching bands as they pace by, employees know it's coming. The first signs are subtle, like safety posters and production results suddenly appearing on the walls, or the boss seen uncharacteristically wandering around the building idly chatting with the workers. Other signals are more obvious, like flowers appearing in the lobby, landscaping activity near the building entrance, or repairs made to equipment and work areas that had been in disrepair for months. And then, there is "the memo," left on every desktop from a suddenly stressed out manager confirming the rumored visit and "reminding" them to clean their work areas and make a neat appearance.

The parade is coming to town.

Messes...And Other Opportunities

In monarchic organizations, the more that the bosses make of the upcoming parade, the less employees look forward to the event. Many secretly hope for that eagerly awaited embarrassing moment that finally exposes their bosses for what they are—managers without names on their doors—and gives them the treatment they have long deserved. After all, employees know that little is going to change for the better as long as the local bosses are able to cover up the deficiencies that need to be systemically fixed, not cosmetically covered up. They also know that when the parade is over that the only thing left behind will be the mess, and they know who will be responsible for cleaning it up, even if they didn't create it.

Conversely, in muralistic organizations the leaders and their teams are eager for the opportunity to be "seen" because they are ready and waiting to be discovered. There is no need to dress up their place before the marching band arrives. Nor is there the need of a reminder to suit up and look sharp for the inspection. They have little time to slow down for superficial trivialities. The future will arrive sooner than the parade.

How Does My Job Make Me Feel About Me?

There is another significant difference in these organizations, and it involves a sense of security and control. When monarchs greet the bosses, they do it privately to preserve, protect, and defend their status and to provide the visiting dignitary with their appropriate self-serving "spin," before taking them on the tour of the operation. However, their lack of "the Feel" for their people and social insecurities are quickly revealed as they struggle to identify their employees by name and are stressed to provide a single detail about their families or personal lives. Employees are simply introduced as, "Ray, who has been with us for a few years in the machine shop."

As the parade moves on, the boss is looking for the next name plate, while "Ray," a veteran employee, faces the grim reality that he is just another faceless grunt whose value to the organization is unknown to either his boss or himself. When any opportunity comes his way, he is out of there, and without a moment of regret.

Conversely, muralists have their teams accompany them to their meeting with the boss. The muralist not only introduces each team member, but also provides a complimentary profile of each. There is humor, laughter, and obvious warmth among team members. It takes only a few moments for the boss to understand that something is "different" about them and that something positive is happening as a result. The discussion revolves around projects that "we" are working on and solutions they are developing together.

Team members are given their opportunity to present their piece, display their knowledge, and show their passion and ability. The muralist beams in support, confident and secure in knowing that their ability to prepare the next generation of muralists makes them all more valuable to the organization, and better prepared for their next challenges. The muralists-in-training love their work and admire their leader, because their job and their boss make them feel better about themselves. They are well aware that their better opportunities and best days are in front of them.

However, muralists do share one thing in common with monarchic organizations. They both want the big bosses to understand what's really going on. The difference is in their sense of perspective.

Why And Because

Still, the news of the upcoming parade tends to provoke more panic than promise, which leads to yet another question. "Why is negativity so often expressed toward management?" Most employees would probably say that the explanation is pretty simple and based on the old maxim, "Because they have earned it." Sadly, there is often more truth in this than understood by the visiting executives. Consider these not uncommon scenarios:

- After being advised of the VIP visit and preparing accordingly, executives enter and exit the premises without stopping at the desks and workstations of the rank and file to shake a hand or offer thanks for their service.
- When addressing the work force, the executive is so bland that the employees feel neither inspired nor impressed.
- The VIPs act bored or disinterested or threatening when they answer questions, or otherwise make it clear that they are paid to see the big picture, not specific operations or even the people.

Under any such scenario it doesn't take very long before the employees' reactions to the parade are known. The people know the difference between being managed and being led. Managers who reveal themselves to be "insincerely insincere" (or even worse—arrogant) are quickly and summarily labeled as "empty suits" and discounted as disappointing at best or untrustworthy at worst.

Leaders who are perceived as more sincere receive a positive response. However, a favorable impression does not necessarily mean that employees are instantly or easily impressed by a potential leader either. After all, the Trojan Horse trick worked only once. Years of experience have built up so much cynicism and scar tissue relating to management that employees want to see the actual proof of benefits in action before they lower their defenses, expose their emotions, and make their commitment to someone else or something new.

And yet, organizations press forward, overloading their undersized airplanes with new initiatives and old baggage, without sufficiently explaining why they are needed or how their work forces will benefit. How can they so carelessly ignore the traditional barriers of organizational resistance, or think that employees do not remember the last layoff or "miscommunication," or have forgotten the past disasters from failed initiatives that have created a confidence gap with management?

Is there any reason to disbelieve that "the plane" won't crash in the same place again this year?

"What You Think You Heard Is Not What I Think I Said"

What this means is that if there is a new strategic change in direction, or even just a slightly different message that will adversely affect the workforce, the "cultural caution light goes on." In these situations, managers must lead by taking their program out on the road and persuasively making (not marketing) their case to the very people who must deliver on its potential. It cannot be done (as is too often attempted) by memo or by a surrogate, because the message "received" will be far different from the one intended. It begins with the identity and credibility of the messenger.

And, don't expect that the message will be successfully communicated in a single session. The workforce is looking for a consistent message over time, before jumping at the latest "flavor of the month" from the ivory tower. Therefore, implementing a strategic initiative or a procedural change is more about preparing for a marathon than a quick sprint that is over before anyone notices that anything is different. The people are far too smart for that and their memories are too long.

Unfortunately, most managers do not sufficiently understand that this creates a significant personal responsibility and commitment on their part. Too few managers are willing, and even fewer are capable of matching their energy and ability to lead against the considerable emotional force of the rank and file to resist. Therefore, as often happens, when managers lose their interest, or move on to something new before the outstanding initiative is effectively operational, they are shocked to later learn that employees have reverted to their original behavior, "until someone with authority can get their message straight." You can close your eyes and see the finger pointing and blame gaming from here, but in the end it all comes back to a failure to lead.

The bottom line is that it all begins at the top. Employees are very impressed by leaders who roll up their sleeves, know their business, remember their names, understand their problems, speak empathetically and can explain their vision, objectives and problems openly and plainly—and with an occasional sense of humor.

In short, employees respond positively to leaders who lead, and they will typically do what it takes when the leader is viewed as a person who can identify and relate to them. However, once the leaders stop leading and begin delegating their critical credibility roles to their lieutenants, belief turns to betrayal and the "top" soon becomes an arrogantly dispassionate place. From the employees' vantage point, it's Caesar redux, and the Ides of March can't come soon enough.

So, getting the correct message delivered by the right messenger is a big deal, and yet companies mess this up more often than they seem to get it right. A state of confusion soon reigns and the infrastructural resistance begins. How many times have you sat in a meeting and heard someone conclude that (in best "Cool Hand Luke" fashion) "What we have here is a failure to communicate?"

At some point in their careers, everyone has heard the boss retreat from a well-understood commitment by saying something utterly bizarre such as, "What you think you heard is not what I think I said." In monarchic organizations, this happens not infrequently, probably because they still do not understand that their people are their primary assets (in real, not rhetorical, terms). If they did, would they so consistently discount them or take them for granted?

Picasso vs. Rockwell

Part of the disconnection lies in the significantly different views of the world between management and the workforce. They are as different as their interpretations of "art."

To the monarchic ivory tower crowd looking out from the proverbial 30,000 feet, the art of the earth below resembles a Picasso—a mosaic of neatly sculptured shapes and boundless resources, perfectly patterned and seamlessly quilted together with endless time and limitless potential, flexibly interchangeable, continually redefinable, and readily adaptable to organizational needs.

However, the art of the workforce on the ground is like a Rockwell—imperfect, earth toned, wrinkled, uneven and human, pockmarked with drop dead deadlines, inadequate direction, insufficient tools, and limited possibilities, all uncontrollably predetermined by the faceless names of executives looking down from "on high."

No wonder so many organizations have a difficult time getting it right. They don't always see the same picture.

Another distinction rests with the different view of the organizational world by monarchs and muralists.

- **Muralists** refer to their people by their names.
  monarchs reference people as "head counts";
- **Muralists** see their people as *assets* of appreciating value and the key differentiator of their organization's competitive advantage.
  monarchs label their head counts as "resources," synonymous with computers or pencils or paper clips, and just as depreciable and routinely disposable.

How do you want to be valued by your organization—as an asset or a resource?

In taking "the king can do no wrong" attitude, monarchs fail to consistently understand that they have an accountable role within their organizations—to develop the strategy and provide the tools that allow their "head counts" to productively do their jobs. Unless they deliver on that responsibility, the credibility gap between the bosses and the bossed will continue, and the saying, "We're from Corporate and we're here to help you" will remain as one of the three great lies.

Muralists have a different idea. They are confident to initiate the call to Corporate, to show and tell them why they are very excited about what they are doing, to share their enthusiasm and results, and to ask for Corporate's input to help them do even better or to even pass their practice forward to others.

When the parade arrives as a result of this kind of a call, break out the balloons! Everybody loves that kind of a parade.

CHAPTER 13

Pacman Is Life

"The monarch resorts to the traditional 'my way or the highway'...The muralist says, 'We're going to a new and better place, follow me and I will help you get there...'"

How do mentor-leaders emerge to bridge the cultural gaps which separate the bosses from the bossed?

Just as in the case of working with children, some of life's answers can be found in unexpected places. For instance, managers can also develop "the Feel" for leading in a nontraditional setting, like an arcade, just as readily as they can in the more clinical setting of a classroom, and "the answer" may be available for only a quarter.

For instance, let's consider the "meaning" and metaphorical value of Pacman! Did you ever wonder why there was such a universal and intergenerational appeal regarding this video game? Even when the arcades were not filled with people, and vacant machines just begged for quarters, people of all ages waited in line eager to play Pacman. Why did this game reach such a broad cross section of Americana?

Perhaps it is the simple, but (at least) subliminal, premise of the game, and the obvious metaphor de vie.

The "Game" Continues Until It's "Over"

The game features the Pacman, a video "Everyman", doing his humble job gathering pellets and minding his own business. However, when "the boss

73

man" determines that he is not moving quickly enough, the ghosts are discharged to bite him in the butt to "motivate" him to do his job faster, to be more efficient in the process, and to "remind" him who's boss.

The good news is that better players are able to swallow strategically located power pills, giving them the opportunity to turn the tables on their pursuers. The bad news is that their advantage is only temporary and the situation (too) quickly reverts to "normal." The Pacman is soon back in his rat race, stressed out and ducking and dodging his way through the maze in constant fear of his survival.

Skilled players who successfully gather up all the pellets with their senses still intact, are promoted to higher levels—with faster ghosts and fewer exits. The "game" continues until "it's over." It's a tough game. Most players fail to reach the higher levels before they are summarily replaced at the controls by another player.

Does this sound familiar?

Pacman was probably invented by monarchs to reinforce the issue of control and institutionalize the concept of the monarchy. The game was and remains successful because everyone, at least subliminally, understands that "Pacman is life." This is how the game is played between the bosses and the bossed.

While employees clearly relate to the Pacman, few bosses see themselves as the ghosts, and even fewer understand their need or responsibility to exorcise the demons from the workforce to help their workers be successful. Consequently, generations of monarchic managers perpetuate the practice that the best way to "motivate" employees is to continually bite them in the butt and threaten a negative performance review. In the process, they fail to understand that they demotivate their employees from working up to their potential. This is especially true for their best workers who have other employment options and increasingly exercise them, while institutionalizing organizational resistance to management and strategic changes.

At some point along the way, the arrogance of Caesar will recur beyond the bounds of tolerance. Some monarchs will be "mortally wounded" by the most daring and skilled Pacmen, waiting in the weeds and aching for an opportunity for retribution, with power pills at their sides and a sense of revenge in their hearts. Few tears will be shed when the lids of their boxes slam shut.

The Bus Is Leaving

For any organization that needs the contributions from their entire workforce to be successful, the method that managers use to get everyone productively engaged in the process is critical, and helps to further define the difference between monarchs and muralists.

Every organization has its share of star "Pacman" players who immediately understand the objectives, readily adapt to organizational changes, and reach higher performance levels faster than the others. A second tier of employees is more cautious, but also "gets it" quickly especially after they see that it is "safe" to try. However, there is usually a small group of employees (the third tier) that either has difficulty adjusting, or simply refuses to seek or even rejects coaching. They cannot seem to get beyond the first level or two before succumbing or quitting—or worse, unproductively going through the motions under the radar scope.

After any change, organizations have more people in this tier than they realize because managers are too easily enamored by the early adapters who "prove" that their plan is successful. They never seem to see (or conveniently ignore) the silent minority of stragglers who are haunted by the ghosts of traditional behavior and scared to death by the new ghosts at their door.

"We Are Taking A Trip To A Better Place"

Monarchs believe that success is a choice, as if it is a self-determining option, and that people who are slow to adapt are simply choosing to be unsuccessful. They will soon become frustrated by their stragglers and declare that ready or not, "the bus" is leaving. The message is clear enough, but in their hormonal desire to execute their power and exert their control, there is a need to understand if monarchs are sufficiently aware of the increasingly higher costs related to demotivating their workforces. This includes dispiriting their most capable employees who may be on board this time, yet realize that they are there without their friends, and know that they may be only one game board away from their own demise (unless they reach the exit first).

Muralists, on the other hand, will take a different approach. Because they work from the back of the maze, they know the final destination and understand when their bus will depart, where the bus is headed, and what has to be done to get their people ready to go. The communication to their workforce will be clear, direct, supportive, and timely:

- the bus will be leaving soon
- we will be going to a different, but interesting place
- we will be blazing a new trail
- we will be developing new answers to old questions
- we will train and prepare you to be on board
- ...but you need to help make yourself ready to go.

What a difference in their approach!

- **Muralists** paint a picture in bold colors and subtle tones so that everyone can see the objective and find their way to the destination; *monarchs* resort to the traditional "my way or the highway" routine, and send a clear signal to employees, "Release the ghosts!"

- **Muralists** understand that the ghosts will always have the upper hand until their team develops a new strategy to defeat them;
  monarchs make employees feel like insecure Pacmen needing to conform or be defeated.
- **Muralists** have their feet on the ground, focused on preparing their people to find new answers to old questions to successfully complete the mission;
  monarchs interpret shapes from 30,000 feet, fixating on the mission and not the people.
- **Muralists** appreciate their assets;
  monarchs depreciate their resources.
- **Muralists** receive commitment;
  monarchs demand compliance;
- **Muralists** encourage them until they soar;
  monarchs make employees march until they're sore.

By the way, the bus drivers for the trip are the mentor-leaders. They know about Caesar and the schoolyard. Their pockets are filled with quarters so they can play in the game, share what they have learned, remain connected to their people, and be increasingly relevant to the mission.

Which would you prefer—to get your ticket punched, or to receive a ticket to ride?

CHAPTER 14

The Organizational Swiss Watch

"Muralists make their employees feel better about themselves and their contributions to the organization. When employees are turned on, everything happens on time because the gears are well aligned and the attitudes are finely tuned. In exchange, they do not want to fail or disappoint their leader, and seldom do."

Is your organization "running like a Swiss watch" or does it look more like a piece of Swiss cheese?

A generation ago, the Swiss watch was the standard of precision. While quartz movements and digital time are everywhere these days, this long-time metaphor for quality remains equally valid when you look at the multitude of moving parts of an exposed chronometer. Inside you can see the skillfully designed and intricately engineered assemblage of moving wheels of varying sizes, all working together to provide a perfect product—the precise time.

Tucked away to the rear of the timepiece, but moving very rapidly, are the little wheels. The movements gradually increase in size closer to the front, but appear to move progressively slower, all the way up to the biggest wheel which hardly seems to move at all. Of course, the irony is that the slowest moving wheel is connected to the hands, which provide the "product" that everyone needs, and the melodious chiming that everyone appreciates.

It's Synchronization That Matters, Not Size

It seems "unfair" for the littlest wheels to be going like the hubs of hell while the biggest wheels appear to be "doing nothing," yet taking all the credit. However, the design of the chronometer requires that every wheel *be* interconnected and *move* in synchronization. Each wheel has its own specific role, but none can work in isolation. Hence, when one wheel slows, they all slow and the timing is thrown off; when one breaks down, the entire operation comes to a halt, time stops and the chimes don't ring.

The comparison to an organization is not hard to make.

The metaphor is all the more compelling in that organizations are able to run like the proverbial Swiss watch only when the roles and responsibilities (e.g., jobs) of the workforce are as precisely structured, interconnected, and aligned. This means that the big wheels must provide the vision, strategy, direction, and leadership; the medium-sized wheels must understand the vision and strategy, then implement the tactics to carry out its objectives; and the little wheels must be designed and finely tuned to operationally execute to the plan.

Design, process, communication, feedback, and synergy form the lifeblood of the organizational structure. Therefore, when those wheels are out of sync, the organization will never be on time. If time is money, then the only conclusion that can be made in most organizations is that a lot of it is being wasted, due to the failure to successfully execute.

There is obviously a big difference between the Swiss watch and the Swiss cheese. One is a precision instrument made to be handed down through generations; the other is full of holes, with a limited shelf life. Hence, in organizations where the mission, vision, strategy, and people are in alignment, there is a strong likelihood for success. However, for organizations that are flawed by unclear objectives, poor system and process design, and dysfunctional wheels, their demise will likely predate the terms of their leased space.

Roles and relationships within organizations are by neccessity interdependent, yet this is a difficult organizational concept for many companies to adopt, implement or successfully manage. Ultimately, most failures will resurrect the standard "breakdown in communication" excuse, instead of the real reasons that are clearly reflected in the corporate mirror—their inability to design an efficient system, or execute within it, caused by the failure of their leaders to effectively lead.

The Time Of Your Life

What do you "see" when you look at the clock on the wall—your organization or just the time; an intrically designed work of art made to last or a lily pad laden operation chronically running out of time? An introspective assessment is critical, to understand the difference.

Monarchs often do not understand how their operations fit into the larger, holistic picture, or do not care. Their principle objective is to tightly control their little "box" and to "not look bad" in front of their boss. As a result, monarchs tend to see only their "wheel" of responsibility and are aggressively protective when challenged by anyone encroaching on their turf, or perceived to be gaining an "advantage" at their expense. Over time, they become masters at the blame game, even if their actions reduce organizational efficiency or lower overall results.

Consequently, organizations that spawn multiple, semi-independent fiefdoms create petty internal competition and interesting office politics, but they cannot effectively compete against more coordinated rivals. They delude themselves into thinking that they are following the rules and staying within the lines, while actually creating an inefficient form of intramural anarchy.

In organizations where this circumstance prevails, it is quite apparent that the organizational dynamics have come unglued and there is little or no effective leading going on. It's as though all the wheels are spinning independently but everyone thinks that because they are working up a sweat, they are doing their jobs. That's like telling the time by looking only at the big hand. The net effect is that the organization functions dysfunctionally because the gears are not meshing. The well-engineered chronometer model was trashed long ago by dueling feudal lords fiercely competing for what most certainly will become a diminishing return from a smaller, if not totally disappearing, piece of the cheese.

The Muralistic Chronometer - A Horological Sacrament

Muralists, however, see the clock as a horological sacrament—an outward and visible sign of a symbiotic and organizational thing. They clearly understand and are capable of communicating the interdependencies of the mission, vision, strategy, objectives, tactics, and operations to their workforce—and how they fit into the broader picture. They create a trusting environment that stays "on time" because their people stay in tune with one another and because their successes are mutual and interconnected.

Muralists, including their "muralists-in-training," worry less about the constraints of time and think more in terms of transforming their project vision into a tangible reality. They see hours as units to be stretched to allow them to meet their deadlines, and make their mark. Because they are passionate about their work, they come in early, stay late, and work on weekends—doing whatever it takes—and without being asked or told. Everyone knows what needs to be done and when it must be completed—and they do it without laborious discussions of job descriptions or the length of the workweek.

They love all their "todays," but they also can't wait for tomorrow to see what's next.

These cultures revolve around their muralistic mentor-leaders, to whom the people are fiercely loyal. There are many reasons for this, but the most significant is really the most simple. Muralists make their employees feel better about themselves and their contributions to the organization. When employees are turned on, everything happens on time because the gears are well aligned and the attitudes are finely tuned. In exchange, they do not want to fail or disappoint their leader, and seldom do.

Paper Handcuffs

It's a particularly interesting phenomenon to see the two differently managed groups of employees working in close proximity. The monarch group may not voluntarily support the idea of working long or late, but they privately envy the passion, commitment, and confidence that the muralists exude; and the appreciation they receive from their leader, even as they gossip about those "stuck up elitists across the hall."

However, few will dare to take the risk of transferring into the muralist group because they have been so deconditioned ("paper handcuffed") into conformity by monarchs. They fear that they don't have the "stuff" to compete or excel in a more demanding environment. After all, it's easier and less personally taxing to put in your time, complain about the boss, and hope for a promotion when the monarch retires in five years, than to voluntarily sign on for projects that will create even temporary discomfort and expose them to a learning curve. In short, they are in their "comfort zone," comfortably comfortable knowing what they know and doing what they do, but zoned out of taking personal risk, let alone daring to be different.

To Muralists, Anything And Everything Is Possible

Muralists are certainly well aware of their longer hours, frenetic moments beating deadlines, and time spent in empty offices, lonely hotel rooms, and faraway airports. But they also believe that they are members of an elite unit on a definable mission. They are empowered and turned on by their accountability because it makes them feel "alive" and necessary and relevant. They clearly understand and firmly believe that they are learning at a far faster rate than those less committed or accountable, and that this makes them more valuable to their organization. More importantly, with each new success they gain self-confidence and expand their faith in themselves, their leader, and their team. As far as "getting it done" is concerned, "anything and everything is possible," because they deliver it daily and they do it together.

While they may occasionally feel the strain associated with pressure packed, high-exposure projects, they would never think for a moment of changing places with anyone in the monarch groups. That would be the equivalent of moving from the land of the living to the land of the living dead, and they choose not to be prematurely placed in the box. The good news, of course, is that a person's liberation and ascension to the role of "muralist" is like commencement—the beginning of their new life as a mentor-leader. There is no going back. Few would even want the option.

This year, instead of giving away a holiday "turkey," give your managers a wall chronometer with the moving parts exposed and a written description of how an organization works. If your managers cannot read the "writing on the wall," or begin demonstrating more muralistic qualities, give them a pound of Swiss, a roll of quarters, and send them to the arcade to play Pacman until they can figure "it" out.

CHAPTER 15

What's The Story?

"There are really only two primary components to the (business) story, 'the aroma and the cake.' The aroma creates the initial customer attraction, but the quality of the cake either brings them back or keeps them away."

Another key distinction between organizations that are run like a Swiss watch and those that smell more like a piece of "flawed fromage," is their story and the ability of their managers to proudly and passionately tell it.

There are really only two primary components to the story, "the aroma and the cake." The aroma creates the initial customer attraction, but the quality of the cake either brings them back or keeps them away.

Of course, to tell the story managers first need to know it and understand what it's all about. You would think that knowing the story would be the easy part since managers typically spend more time at work than they do at home.

However, in many organizations even the slightest scent of the story (assuming one even exists) is typically neither well known, nor well understood. Many managers don't know it, can't tell it, or (even worse) don't believe it. Without their knowledge and support, or the ability to communicate the story to the workforce, the organizational grapevine and rumor mill fill the void. When the story becomes a "fill in the blanks" type of condition, the aroma usually smells, and the cake isn't particularly good either. The story, therefore, is not a minor detail. Check out what happens when you don't have all your facts just right:

Which Tire?

Four college students drove a hundred miles to another school for a Saturday night party in the middle of their final exams. However, they drank too much and could not drive back safely to their school, so they "crashed" in a dorm for the night. Unfortunately, by the time they got up the following day, a blizzard had hit the area, leaving them hung over and hung up far away from where they needed to be. By the time they returned to their campus, it was nearly dawn and their final exam was at 8 A.M.

They agreed to tell their professor that they had had a blowout on the interstate, stranding them in the storm for many hours until the Highway Patrol could reach them and get help to repair the tire and enable them to get going. Cold, tired, and without the chance to do last minute cramming, they asked for a makeup exam.

The professor looked them over closely as he listened to their story. He asked a few questions and finally agreed. As they departed, he assured them that they should be very prepared the next morning because their makeup test would be far different from the scheduled exam.

The next day, the professor spaced them widely apart in the auditorium and distributed their tests. The exam had only two questions. The first was a true or false question worth five points which they answered quickly, and turned to the second page which simply read,

"For 95 points, *Which Tire?*"

They were dead in their chairs and they knew it less than a minute into their exam because they didn't have a credible story. The same thing happens every day in business. Presentations are over before they are scarcely underway because there are too few details presented to form a credible story, leaving little reason to listen, and less reason to believe or buy. Just as damaging, but less explainable, is that even when there is a coherent story, there are very few managers who can stand on their feet and convincingly and passionately tell it. This is the equivalent of a newspaper having the "Big Scoop," but not credibly delivering the story to its readers.

When The Crew Pulls Only On The Right Oar...The Organization Goes Nowhere

Muralistic organizations have well-conceived and purposeful missions as well as a clear, consistent, and powerful story. They also have standards, objectives, process, expectations, and well-defined roles for employees that make their story real. In essence, the story becomes the overarching cultural symbol that creates their organizational spirit, passion, and pride. The story unites, binds, and rallies employees to their mission. Muralists can tell their story because they live it, believe it, and because they are proud to be associated with it.

Conversely, monarchic companies have stories that are so full of holes that there are more doubters than missionaries among the managers. Without a credible story an organization has no strategic direction and few true believers. However, lack of direction is the life blood of monarchs because it perpetuates their anarchic competition for control of the hierarchical high ground and allows the story to change with each despot's self-serving version. These organizations are like racing shells, their crews staffed only by monarchs-in-waiting, each pulling hard on the "right" oar, energetically spinning the enterprise in circles, but going nowhere in the process.

Employees are well aware of the internal battles that consume the time and energy of their "leaders," and which sidetrack the organization from its mission. At various times monarchic politics actually provide significant amusement in the lunchroom and at the copy machine.

However, over time the workforce becomes confused, polarized, and ultimately dispirited. This has an even higher "hidden cost" impact than most organizations realize. Poor results ultimately translate into lost jobs for the people who need them the most; and the departure of key employees (e.g., the assets) who the organization needs the most. Employees know this and are all the more frustrated when the organization's obvious potential is squandered by the constant squabbling of its leaders. How can the workforce get passionate about their work in an organization that cannot define itself in terms its people understand or believe? How can a company succeed when their leaders view their primary competition as the monarch in the next office, not the other company across town, or in another country, developing the next latest and greatest product or the better ideas?

"The Look"

If lack of a coherent story is not trouble enough for most organizations, perhaps an equally significant problem is that few managers have the ability to passionately present the story even when one exists.

In the play, *The Master Class*, a story about the life of Maria Callas, an internationally known opera diva, Callas is past her prime as a performer, but is operating a finishing school (e.g., "the Master Class") for rising opera singers. A key scene in the play revolves around the concept of "the Look."

One after another, the up-and-coming performers present their considerable singing skills to the critical scrutiny of the audience and Callas. They are all very talented, but they sound so dispassionately similar that she becomes quickly distracted, stops listening, and lapses into theatrical side trips of her own brilliant performances in front of adoring audiences. When the music stops, the young divas press for her assessment of their talent, almost demanding that she tell them that they will be as great and famous and talented as she had been.

But Callas is a hard sell. She knows greatness when she sees and hears it. She studies them with a critical eye, and then grandiloquently answers to the hushed audience, "You're asking me if people will want to listen to you? You're asking me if you are going to be well-known and famous because you have talent? Well, if you have to ask me if you are going to be good, then I have to tell you that you will never be any good at all, because you don't have 'the Look!'"

The performers are dismayed because they do not understand what she is telling them. They believe that all they need is a fine voice, an attractive appearance, and an appreciative audience. They are wrong! Excellence is more than wearing bold colors and meeting the minimum requirements.

So, what is "the Look," how does it help distinguish a leader from a manager, and how much time does the audience (of employees or customers) wait around to see if you've got the right stuff before they mentally check out, then physically wander off to other things and other problems?

"The Look" Is What It Is—And, It's All About You!

- "The Look" is *not* as much about your ability to sing as it is about your ability to project the message of the song.
- It's *not* about your being present; it's about your presence.
- It's the essence of being a *somebody* in a room full of "somebodies."
- It's about your poise, confidence, knowledge, passion, and ability to convincingly communicate in private meetings, small groups, or large audiences.
- It's not just about the bold colors; it's also about the subtle tones.
- It's not just about being the same as everyone else; it's about confidently daring to be different.

Having "the Look" is a key factor in making you different from all the rest who would gladly pay to possess it. However, "the Look" is not for sale to anyone, no matter how much they would willingly pay.

"The Look" is not defined in the dictionary, but you know what it means when you're in its presence. It doesn't have to be anything as overstated or nebulous as "charisma," it can be as classy and understated as elegance. However it happens or whenever it appears, people respond to it under any form, but they don't confuse it with excessive arrogance, self-righteousness, or extreme egotism.

The important thing about "the Look" is that nobody can prevent you from presenting it to your advantage, or more persuasively strutting your stuff than anyone else. It is what it is, and in the end, it's all about *you*. But, it doesn't exist in a vacuum.

However, in all organizations there are risks associated with being known as someone who has "the Look." Monarchs negatively and enviously characterize these up-and-coming threats as being counter culturalists deviating from the traditional procedures, or rebels "marching to their own drummer." Such criticisms quickly discourage the faint of heart and weak of knee, and keep the least secure souls paper handcuffed to conformity—but not the true muralistic believers. They see what they see, and what they see is that many people are drawn to, and even seek out leaders possessing "the Look." And when these leaders look at the faces that are looking back at them, they are looking at faces filled with the hope that this time "it's different" because, at last, they are in the presence of somebody who actually is *different* because they get "it" and they possess the ability and the presence to give *it* back.

Even when words are not spoken (and they usually aren't), muralists understand the commitments that are being asked and accepted—both ways. This establishes a compellingly energetic leadership continuum— visionary leaders with an inspirational message and the ability to passionately communicate it; working with motivated followers who eagerly accept personal risk to overcome hierarchical and cultural obstacles to find new answers to old questions; which in turn (re)invigorates their committed leaders whose greatest fear is failing their followers; which re-commits their followers whose greatest fear is failing their leader, etc.

They feed on each other's hopes and dreams, skills and energies, and passions and commitments to one another. When this happens to any group or organization, it's magic!

But A "Good Look" Can Appear Bad…To Monarchs

Therefore, it's little wonder why competing monarchs fear the intangible power flowing to those who have got "it," even in the absence of the formalized authority to possess it. While they are skilled at competing for hierarchical turf, they can neither inspire nor motivate their people with the same conviction, passion, vision, and confidence of the muralists who are living (and telling) their story. As a result, they will seek to dismiss such leaders as superficial or idealistic, or describe their message as rhetoric or fluff. They will construct subtle barriers and organizational roadblocks (e.g., accelerate the down escalator) to impede their progress and even sabotage their projects. Or, they will even resort to moving an "up-and-comer" to a different job to break their momentum and to be placed in a position where they may fail (while being systematically discredited for their previous work), or become so discouraged that they leave the organization.

However, the few among them—the truly "different" ones, with the philosophy, the passion and the relentless strength of their convictions—understand that success comes only if their commitment to succeed is persistent enough to overcome the aggregate resistance of those who do not share their enthusiasm and personal objectives.

This is what separates leaders from managers.

The Path Of Least Resistance Usually Isn't

Compare these business challenges to those of a kick returner in a football game. His job is to work within the plan and to succeed inside the lines. As he stands on the goal line awaiting the ball, he knows that if he runs at full speed directly down the middle of the field, he will achieve his objective precisely one hundred yards and approximately ten seconds later—untouched. He also knows that he cannot do it alone, which is why the coach has designed, and the team has practiced, a strategy to make the plan happen.

Of course, the competition is equally committed to succeeding and they have very different plans of their own. Somewhere, between the philosophy and reality of the competing strategies, the runner is usually tackled short of the goal line.

However, when the returner is successful, he will most likely have had to incorporate a series of unplanned detours, reacted quickly and decisively to sudden, and unexpected events; retained his balance, refrained from fumbling, maintained his composure, avoided devastating hits, and displayed courage under duress. Despite the clarity of the game plan, he will most likely have run 25% further than planned and taken at least 50% longer to "get there."

If it were easy, most everyone could do it. However, few players have the skill, desire, stamina, fortitude, and agility to make it through all the noise and the turmoil.

True muralists and leaders, therefore, cannot be easily discouraged. They must have a "visible" inner confidence and resiliency that is infused within the hearts of their followers. They do this by honestly communicating and conveying their feelings with sincere sincerity to their people.

Employees respond very positively to honesty because trust is often perceived as lacking in many managers. The words of the leader's story, therefore, like those of the gymnastics coach, may be calm and reassuring, but their message is loud and clear, just as their commitment to their people is supportive and strong. When this happens, they are committed to go the distance together, whatever the challenges, whatever the obstacles, whatever the resistance.

Conversely, monarchs make a lot of noise, but their message is old and stale, and is eventually viewed by their staffs as more of the same old insincere insincerity. Their words are too often aimed at tearing down a new idea and too seldom heard in the form of an original thought or a coherent story. It does not take long before their workforce sees them as self-serving task masters for whom loyalty is a one-way street that has a dead end.

The story, and the ability to "live" it and deliver it, are therefore very important. Together, they create the passion and momentum that empower excellent mentor-leaders to energize their people to find the new answers to old questions that define and sustain their competitive advantage.

On the other hand, the lack of a coherent story prevents most companies and managers from moving forward, let alone create a competitive advantage.

Muralist leaders also have "the Look." Their wheels are in sync; their chin straps are buckled. They are eager to carry the ball. They take time to analyze what must be said and take ownership of their story. Their messages are filled with both the bold colors that their assets can visualize and subtle tones that they can feel. There is passion. There is credibility.

When a customer asks the question every member on the muralists's team not only knows "which tire," they also know the rest of the story as well.

As a result, muralists are consistently "lucky." Their customers always come back for another piece of cake.

CHAPTER 16

What's Your Widget?

"...Every employee faces unique moments of truth when the success or failure of their organization hinges upon what they know and what they can do at the very moment they must know it or have to do it."

It's interesting how even relatively obscure events can highlight the presence, or expose the absence, of key leadership qualities like "the Look." Consider the vice presidential debates of past elections for example. In 1988, for whatever value that his relative youth and attractive appearance may have offered to the campaign, Dan Quayle, the Republican candidate, simply did not have "the Look" as much as he and his handlers tried to project an image that he did. The people knew better (and usually do).

It would be naïve for managers to doubt that similar observations and evaluations are being gossiped about them every day by their own employees. Unlike Quayle, who was publicly humiliated by his opponent for attempting to be something that he was not, most managers are spared that direct indignity. Their employees typically suffer in silence, enduring their extremes of egotism, arrogance, indifference or ineptitude, while patiently awaiting their "Pacman moment."

An even more troubling metaphor, however, occurred in the following election. This time Quayle was debating Al Gore, the Democratic Party Vice Presidential nominee, along with third-party candidate James Stockdale. Quayle and Gore went after each other like dueling monarchs, totally ignoring their lesser known opponent. Finally, Stockdale broke into "their" debate by asking the critical question, "Why *am* I here?" The obvious absurdity of the question brought laughter to the forum and momentarily focused attention on the unknown candidate. Nevertheless, within moments Quayle and Gore resumed their two-sided attacks as though he was invisible, confirming his irrelevance to the process.

The first story describes a highly public example of why pseudo leaders fail every day. An appealing appearance does not create "the Look," no matter how hard you try to dress it up. The latter story, however, raises an equally interesting, but more compellingly problematic issue. How many employees feel insignificant to their organization and, even after years of experience, remain challenged by the question, "Why am I here" within the context of their roles, responsibilities, and relevance to the organization's strategy?

The Widget—Was Pogo Right?

When there is neither a story nor an identifiable strategy, employees do not readily understand either their place in the organization or the value of what they produce. If you don't believe this, assemble a group of employees at any level of the organization and ask them this simple question, "What's your widget?"

What do employees do or produce to make their organizations distinctive in the marketplace, to provide the value that creates the story that sustains the company's profitability, and to ensure the ongoing need for their employment? Otherwise said, do employees sufficiently understand how their wheel interconnects with the other wheels that, in their aggregate, produce the organization's "end product"?

And, can they tell the story about it?

If you do ask the question, what you will most likely hear is silence, and the silence will be shared equally among new and more highly tenured employees alike. What you will definitely see are people looking at the floor, or up at the ceiling, or even at one other, but *not* at you, each seeking some form of divine inspiration to answer something they know they should know, but don't.

Sadly, Pogo was right. The "enemy" is often the image reflected in the corporate mirror, and Stockdale's comment was more typical than you might think (and definitely more than you can afford).

For the most part, employees, including managers, have not made the connection that, as measured by what they produce or fail to produce compared with their competitors, they are the definable differences of their organizations. *They* are the widget. Nevertheless, in monarchic organizations, despite the fact that they make numerous decisions on their jobs every day, most employees have been so devalued, so tightly controlled, so dispirited, and so uninformed that they do not know or appreciate the criticality of their roles.

Resources vs. Assets

The reason for this may be as subtle, yet insidious, as their being continually referenced as "resources" that subliminally initiates, then perpetuates, their ambivalence toward their managers and employers. Perhaps if they were more frequently and sincerely described as the corporate assets who create the organization's competitive advantage, they would behave differently, and more readily make the connection between their work, their widget, and the organization's results.

This frame of reference is not insignificant. Whether they are the leader devising a strategy, or a manager implementing the plan, or a little wheel figuring out the optimal connecting points to the next wheel in the production chain, every employee faces unique moments of truth when the success or failure of their organization hinges upon what they know and what they can do, at the very moment when they must know it or have to do it.

Developing employees to think clearly and function effectively under duress, when the answers aren't routine and help is hard to find are key measures of leadership. This is why the widget and the story are so critical. When organizations do not have a story, or when their people don't understand their roles within it, they will not consistently or purposefully execute, because they cannot answer the critical question, "Why am I here?"

Through the process of "muralizing" and visualizing the "Rorschach on the wall," muralists do not make this mistake, which is why they are magnets for people who value their work, understand why they are there, and want to make a difference in the mission of the organization.

The Gravity "Phenomenon"

Another of the unintended consequences resulting from the absence of a story or strategy is that managers often fail to understand that they are also responsible for producing a widget! Their widget is to train, develop, and enable their subordinates to produce their widget.

This should not be a difficult concept to grasp. However, instead of leading, motivating, or even nurturing employees, many managers continue to do the familiar jobs of their past while ignoring the current developmental needs of the subordinates they are presumably managing (all the while complaining that their people aren't up to their jobs because they do not do them as well as *they* can).

Others become master delegators and "cover your ass" experts by perfecting the "gravity phenomenon." This is an environment in which fault (and responsibility) flows down hill until it gets to the defenseless person *at the end of the line* who will ultimately be "blamed." Monarchs of this mode find clever (and not so subtle) ways to become "ghosts," covering their flanks by kissing the pampered asses of the monarchs above, and biting the "underproductive" (and unprotected) butts of the Pacmen below.

The bottomline is pretty clear. When all the "wheels" do not sufficiently understand their roles in the widget production line, they become dysfunctional, fall out of sync, waste time, and create a competitive disadvantage (unless their competitors are even more dysfunctional).

That's My Story And I'm Sticking To It...

Without widgets, there is no story. Without a story, there is no strategy. Without a widget, a story, or a strategy, there is little an organization can credibly offer to remain as a business. With all that is known about highly successful companies, you would think that it would be a priority for organizations to either internally develop or externally recruit leaders who are able to establish a competitive advantage by:

• Identifying their organization's widget
• Creating a strategy and story around their widget
• Making the story and the strategy real to their people ("Why am I here?")
• Executing like a Swiss watch.

Leading companies have learned this and pay great attention to the details.

Losing organizations seemingly aspire to a level of mediocrity, then declare "victory" when they have "achieved" minimal objectives. After all, there is nothing like "soaring like an eagle" over a low bar for instant gratification, even if the future viability of the enterprise is in doubt.

Of course, if running a profitable business were easy there would be as many editions of management books on bookstore shelves as there are versions of the Bible. However, achieving success isn't easy, and it has as much to do about luck as it takes to become a twelve point buck. The better you are; the luckier you get. Nevertheless, monarchic organizations continually attempt to cram five pounds of historical nonsense into a four pound sack, and wonder why the only breakthrough they can discover rests at their feet. The final act is to rationalize their poor results and bad luck by telling the three great lies:

1. Our competitors are having similar problems.
2. Our competitors are having even worse results.
3. Our company is better positioned for the future.

Indeed, the last time we got the word, those same managers were still trying to cram those three caribou into that under powered plane, while other managers were still counting lily pads in their sleep.

The Top Of The Hill?

Monarchs preside over most organizations because they control the bureaucracy. They have history, tradition, experience, and fear on their side, along with a rolodex of royalists who have received past promises, and a list of future supplicants with their hands outstretched. They own the top of the hill and are tough to dislodge even if they don't have a coherent story or a workforce of motivated widget makers.

Their positions are further supported by employees who are very familiar with, and are most comfortable within a hierarchical structure, despite its flaws, because it provides stability and order. They may not know their widget, but they do know how "things" work and have become experts at multi-tasking—obeying the boss while counting the months and years until their next promotion or retirement.

However, despite all their power, monarchs do not control the more enlightened and independent thinkers who are more devoted to developing a better widget than kissing the monarch's ring. Consequently, better candidates may be by-passed for leadership positions in favor of less qualified, but more obedient contenders. Therefore, moving up within this type of infrastructure is very difficult for muralists without the blessing of a more forward thinking monarch, or at least one who can use a freer thinker as a lightning rod to assail a rival.

When they do get the chance, muralists are often precariously positioned, at least initially, on the edge of the corporate culture and placed in harm's way by being introduced as a creative thinking "change agent." If there were ever a code phrase for generating cultural resistance, change agent is an organizational bullseye. What it means is that when up and coming muralists get their opportunity, they had better not look down, because there is no safety net for a muralist out on a limb. And, they had better not look behind them either because they may see a monarch with a hacksaw in their hands!

This kind of environment makes it difficult for muralists to recruit followers since only the most highly confident, highly motivated, and passionate people are attracted to such an entrepreneurial environment with inherently more personal risk. Fortunately it does not take many muralists to make a difference.

But Uneasy Lies The Head...

Accepting risk is the typical condition by which muralists gain their opening to strut their stuff and express their theories of advanced widgetry in live combat, in prime time, and in full view of highly placed people. Despite the challenge, they are comfortable with this risk, because muralists want no part of the status quo "guarantees" meted out by a monarch. For muralists, guarantees are too controlling, constraining, and confining. They allow too little latitude to inject a new philosophy into the existing hierarchical order.

Like their patron spirit, Don Quixote, they must be able to overcome the obstacles of traditional behavior and the inevitable internal competitive pressures as they quest forward. After all, when the organizational resistance comes in the form of "But, we have always made our widgets this way," the muralistic leader must be persistently insistent and patiently persuasive in demanding that it is in the organization's best interest to find a different (better) way to get the job done before their competitors get there first. After all, the objective is to "celebrate" success, not to be trapped in a monastery of retro management.

Therefore, when they have the opportunity to shine, muralists must make their mark, and fast, by helping others "see" what they see—new answers to old questions, and a different path on which to find them.

Making it easier for muralists to succeed, however, are their basic tool and skill sets. Muralists have "the Look" and possess "the Feel" for leading. They have a story and can passionately tell it; they can help people visualize what it looks like, how it will happen, and how they will feel when they are successful! In short, their people clearly understand the answer to the key question, "Why am I here?"

Without being asked or told, their people view them as different, primarily because they feel differently about themselves and their jobs than those with "Stockdalitis," because they know why they are doing them. This is what helps them attract and develop loyal followers. Working together, their organization delivers the widgets that make their story really real, really fast.

Along the way, they also incubate a new group of muralists-in-training who are eager to rid themselves of the restrictive controls of the "by the numbers" monarch environment, to play to win under different rules and to become leaders pursuing their own "impossible dreams"—but this time with a real chance of achieving them.

Beware Of The Ides Of March...And The Trojan Horse Too

Still, the risk and reward for the intellectual high ground can be contentiously high for muralists, especially if it appears that an upstart manager is not sufficiently subservient or suitably respectful of authority. Monarchs understand power and will use it to protect their position if they feel sufficiently threatened. Conversely, there is nobody more "grateful" than a monarch who benefits from a new approach, suggesting that despite their differences there is nothing that encourages forward thinking like success. This is especially true when someone else has taken the risk and pulled the laboring oar, and where the boss gets the credit.

Nevertheless, once they have had the opportunity to digest the results, monarchs will declare or rationalize that they had blessed the fine art of advanced "widgetry" all along. You'll be astonished to learn that they had created the appropriate environment for creative people "to think out of the box" and deliver a new solution. Alas, it's remarkable how adaptable monarchs can become when it is safe or opportune. And it's equally unforgivable how quickly they can convert a positive into a negative to discredit, then dispose of the "resident rebel," when they are no longer of value, or they think that nobody will notice, and even fewer will care.

Therefore, beware of the Trojan Monarch. The monarchs who giveth, can also taketh away, and often do when the going gets rough, or they feel as though they are losing control or prestige, or their self-interest is better served by something new or somebody else.

Muralistic mentor-leaders may make it look "easy," but they must be mentally tough and totally committed to persevere through the adversity they will face. When their moment comes, they must realize that "carpe diem" means that if they indeed dare to be different, they must be mentally prepared to go the distance, often with only their mirror and most loyal followers to help them get there.

Ask these questions, then hold your breath.

- "What's your widget?"
- "What's our story?"
- "Why are you here?"

If you are not confident about the answers you will hear, there's a whole lot of monarching still going on.

CHAPTER 17

Muralists And Other Benevolent Despots

"The manager matters. You are who you are, but once you are the manager, you have to be better than you were."

A major league baseball manager was once asked about the difference between his managing style and managers whose clubs had finished behind his team. His response, "Nice guys finish last," was memorable, if not especially positive. Years later you still hear references attributing a manager's lack of success to their being "too nice."

This leads to the question, "If nice guys finish last, does that mean that the nastiest guys finish first?"

Fortunately not, and like most baseball managers, when his team's fortunes turned bad in subsequent years, he was fired, suggesting that over time he had either evolved into a much nicer guy or that there is something more to managing than just being the rudest guy in town. Still, the perceived need to have the "tough guy, no nonsense" manager attitude permeates the sports scene even today. Disciplinarians are routinely recruited by failing teams to put an end to the "country club" atmosphere presumably responsible for disappointing results (as opposed to ineffective talent management and poor leading).

What If Managers Could Not Use Sports Analogies?

Nevertheless, this perception further suggests that players and employees either can't or won't deliver up to the highest level of their capabilities until a manager with the sensitivity of a jackhammer, and an attitude to match, arrives on the scene to extract the full measure of their talent by publicly provoking them to reach their full potential.

Like it or not, the behaviors of the sports world often carry over to the business environment, as if they were one and the same. So does the vocabulary. It may only seem this way, but if managers could not use sports analogies to make a point, many would probably be challenged to form an intelligible sentence or express a complete thought. This is acceptable, perhaps, when comparing a home run to a good result, but problematic when a more thought provoking activity is required, like choosing a leader. After all, leading is serious business, not to be minimized by the selection of a sports page-like caricature best known for demeaning their players and offending everyone else with their boorish behavior.

Take the following story of the eager to please bride as an example.

You Scrambled The Wrong Egg

After their honeymoon, the new bride decided to make breakfast for her husband, so she poached an egg and waited for his reaction. He appreciated her effort but told her that he probably would have preferred a scrambled egg instead. The next day she scrambled an egg. He told her that ordinarily he would prefer a scrambled egg, but the poached egg the day before was so delicious he had been hoping for another. The next day, she poached an egg, but the husband chided her for not preparing it the day before when he was in the mood.

This continued for several months. Not surprisingly, the bride became increasingly dissatisfied. Finally, she had a brainstorm. She cooked two eggs, one poached, the other scrambled. She placed covers over each plate, then awaited his reaction. However, when he uncovered the plates and looked at the eggs, he declared, "I can't believe it, you scrambled the wrong egg!"

It's likely that breakfast table will be a very lonely place for him for quite a while, and he has only himself to blame. The odds are pretty good that this monarch wouldn't see a starfish until he stepped on it, and would never think of picking one up. However, the chances are much better that he has an autographed group shot of Pacman's ghosts hanging on his wall.

This does not mean that everyone has to "like" the manager. That's a virtual impossibility. No matter how good they are or how widely they are respected, "Everybody is somebody's [sic] butthead!" However, when somebody is everybody's butthead, "Call Houston" and tell them there's an even bigger problem than they think.

I'll Believe It When I See It
(But, What Will I Do When I Do)?

Why is it that many monarchic managers seem to suffer from premature cynicism? It makes you wonder if it's chronic constipation, or just an advanced form of arrogance that is endemic to monarchs. You can picture the royal highness seated on the "throne," looking down on their resources and snarling, "Go ahead, impress me." Both know the possibility is remote. There are few clues as to what a good job looks like except for the annoyingly vague, "I'll believe it when I see it, but I haven't seen it yet." Sadly, they probably wouldn't know it if they saw it, but even if they did, they would probably do little if anything about it.

Therefore, it doesn't take long for lifters in monarchies to figure out that the most critical measure of success is neither lifting nor leaning. It's also not about excellence either. It's about obedience, and not provoking the boss. After all, why do your best when your best work is not sufficiently differentiated or recognized from anyone else's, no matter how hard you try or how mediocre other work is in comparison?

Companies are filled with employees who must endure this kind of behavior every day from monarchic managers for whom nothing ever seems to be good enough. It's even worse when their behavior places employees in constant fear of losing their jobs unless they kiss up and learn to stop, drop and roll on command. Good widgets become secondary to covered butts. While these monarchs strut about with the sounds of the Rolling Stones humming in their heads, it's their employees who are the ones that "can't get no satisfaction" no matter how hard they try. It's only a matter of time before they move on.

Okay, Now I'll Read It

But what does this say about attitude, management style, and the idea that "nice guys finish last?" Does it really mean (by extension) that "nasty guys finish first?" Are monarchs who utilize a no nonsense, rigidly disciplined, and often despotic approach admired and even revered, because that's what employees really want, expect, and need as their leadership model?

Is This The Best You Can Do?

There is a story attributed to a number of well-known people, including James Michael Curley, the Mayor of Boston in the 1930's, regarding this kind of management style. In the story, the employee submitted a report to Curley then awaited his comments. After a few days of hearing nothing, he asked him if he had read the report. Curley simply replied, "Is that the best you can do?" The employee nervously retrieved his report and worked on it for a few more days before resubmitting it.

More time went by without a response, so he reapproached the Mayor, but was asked the same question, "Is that the best you can do"? Once again he retrieved his report, made some changes and submitted it for a third time. When there was still no reaction, he confronted Curley and asked him about the report. Curley asked the same question, but this time the employee replied, "Yes, that's the best I can do." Curley reportedly replied, "OK, then now I will read it."

The story is actually presented to praise the leadership style and skills of Curley, and the other monarchs to whom the story is "credited." However, what is missed in the translation is that hard-edged monarchs like this establish highly manipulative, one way communication barriers. They manage by fear and intimidation. In these cultures, subordinates are expected to obediently serve monarchs, whatever their level of mental abuse. They hold the salary cards, mete out the bonus awards and decide who gets promoted or let go. The "reward" for employees is more often the avoidance of punishment rather than a pat on the back for doing a good job.

This is a "nice" way for tough guys to lose their heaviest lifters.

Is Turnover An Inevitability Of Organizational Darwinism, Or The Failure To Lead?

However, as offensive a style as this is, many employees, who are summarily ignored, or whose work product routinely disappears into the managerial black hole, would probably gladly take the "Curley treatment." After all, some communication and even negative feedback is better than nothing. It's all a matter of perspective, but it's this kind of negative energy that soon becomes the dominant cultural model throughout the organization. Like the monks, employees wind up copying the wrong models and not engaging in more positive behavior.

The end result is this: if there was such a thing as the "nurturing police," they would be working overtime, yet falling further behind for their effort. While many employees say they want to be "left alone" and allowed to do their jobs, this does not mean that they want to feel (as they often do) that they are in an isolation chamber not knowing what's going on or how well they're doing.

Nevertheless, this trend is increasing through decentralization and the resultant formation of virtual organizations which create virtual relationships with virtual managerial communications, similar to the pretext of "Charlie's Angels" (but without the glamour). When employees are connected by only a laptop and voice mail, they can receive their daily online dose of e-direction and e-criticism from the same faceless people to whom their e-resignations will inevitably be e-directed.

As a result, the leadership bar has never been lower. Monarchs increasingly view employee failures more as a "survival of the fittest" inevitability than as a management failure, even though the failure of leaders to lead plays a significant (and often, dominant) part in the process. The simplistic answer is often to target the more competitive (i.e., "better") schools for replacement candidates, presumably because their graduates are inherently more self-motivated and self-sufficient, and require less time and energy from their managers. It is doubtful that these more expensive candidates have fewer human needs and frailties—or lower expectations—than the people they replace. However, they probably do have more employment options to exercise when their leaders don't provide sufficient communication and support, or fail to measure up to their expectations.

You Are What You Are—Until
You Are The Manager...

All of this highlights one of the basic laws of the schoolyard—the manager matters! You are who you are, but once you are the manager, you have to be better than you were. Unfortunately, this seems to be a fact that continues to be better known to and understood by the followers than the managers.

Whether managers realize it or not, employees watch their comings and goings. They mentally catalogue the best way to get their attention, when they are most accessible, which of their colleagues appear to be favored, where they go to lunch (and with whom), the "nonverbal" gestures they make, their hobbies, interests, corporate connections, personal quirks and habits, quality of wardrobe, tie or shoe collections, and even their walk. They imitate their speech patterns and mock their personal idiosyncrasies. They know which managers support and promote their people and which ones appear to be in it for their own glory. They know which ones are leaders with a ticket to ride somewhere else (and will bring them along), and the ones who are on that midnight train to nowhere (and will take them down with them).

In fact, if managers could anonymously observe a focus group of their assets talking about them, they would be shocked to learn how clearly these perceptions have been made, and how well or poorly they are regarded. Most would probably be embarrassed.

In their desire to establish control, practice discipline, and avoid being a "nice guy," monarchs see the debris, but never the starfish. They do not inspire subordinates to seek out answers to questions that have not been asked, but need to be. They miss the point that communication and confidence building are their responsibilities. They shortsightedly fail to recognize that they will be the direct beneficiary of more capable and higher powered employees—if only they would make a sufficient effort to help them "get there."

Lifters need leaders who will encourage them to achieve to their potential, to inspire a sense of personal dignity, self-confidence, and self-respect, and to help them advance to a higher level of professional development and self-fulfillment. No wonder that the most motivated employees are often the most desperate to escape the monarch's grasp, to seek out muralistic mentor-leaders—or to leave the organziation.

Work Is An Emotional State Of Being

Let's face it, work is an emotional state of being! Employees principally want to earn their pay and find their place in their organizations. They want and need to be supported and appreciated in the process. They also want to believe that there are future opportunities and rewards for them in exchange for their productive work. Instead, many become increasingly disillusioned by their managers until they finally leave after being tormented or ignored beyond the limits of their coping skills.

When these employees do walk out the door, the "royal rationalizations" from the monarchic management are usually the same, "They simply could not cut it;" "They were not tough enough;" "They were too nice;" "They left for more money." Seldom will they say that the real issue was the employee's frustrated inability to "satisfy the unsatisfiable" demands of managers who did not know what they wanted, would not say what they needed, and could not understand what was delivered.

However, fellow employees know otherwise and it just quickens their path to the door before the same thing happens to them. After all, the monarchs invented and perfected the game of Pacman, but skilled players learn that their survival depends on their knowing the locations of the power pellets and the side exits, and getting out of the maze before it's too late.

Are Monarchs "Mr. Tough Guy"... And Muralists Just Fancy Sounding "Mr. Nice Guys?"

But does this simply mean that all monarchs are tough guys who bully their way to success oblivious to their shortcomings and at the expense of anyone in their way? Conversely, does it mean that all muralists are just nice guys, doomed to failure because a head and a heart are weak substitutes for a foot and a fist?

In practice, it is unlikely that either extreme of management "style" can work over the long term. Even when the leader has "star power," they will ultimately fail without a good widget, a relevant story, and a competent strategy. Monarchs without a touch of idealism and a sense of the future will soon become as boorishly irrelevant as muralistic dreamers who pay so much attention to the true, the good and the beautiful, that they forget there is a real game called business underway, and that they are in it.

In the end, organizations cannot be "democracies." Decisions cannot be made by plebiscite. There must be structure to efficiently compete and to effectively survive. Somebody must paddle the kayak and be fully accountable for the promises of the business plan. The leader therefore, must be more than a dreamer, but less than a bully. After all, the widgets must be produced and distributed at a profit for the organization to survive and its talent to remain employed. The wheels must be maintained to move at the appropriate pace, on time, and on budget. This definitely does not happen by luck.

The traditional management structure has been the monarchy. This structure supports power and authority. Orders are issued, and orders are obeyed. Subordinates defer to their superiors, fearful of overextending their levels of authority, and hopeful that they will make a favorable impression worthy of promotion. This is a tough environment in which to be a muralist.

But does this mean that if the monarch were to be summarily displaced by a muralist that the organization would quickly disassemble and "come in last?" Muralists may give this impression by creating an environment of open communication, team building, and group involvement in objective setting and project development. Their constancy of feedback, both positive and constructive, creates energy and enthusiasm among employees. They tend to use a different vocabulary and deploy more supportive methods to produce their widgets. The muralist may even smile and display an optimistic attitude.

However, while there is always "power" connected to leading, in muralistic organizations the most powerful organizational context is the overarching philosophy which connects the leaders with their followers.

It would be a mistake, therefore, to view muralists as any less committed to their philosophy than the more traditional monarchs are committed to retaining their power. In fact, because they are constantly seeking out new answers to old questions, muralists must be more passionately committed to their philosophy, and the ongoing support of their followers ("Why am I here?"), because they must overcome the considerable cultural and hierarchical barriers, and accept personal risk to achieve their objectives.

Over time the structure of the resultant "muralocracy of the motivated" evolves into a "Swiss watch" model which effectively supports the organization's evolving philosophy and not to absolutely serve, protect, and defend the power of the muralist.

Therefore, while they may challenge the conventional wisdom, muralists cannot be anarchic "free agents." They lead differently and more participatively than monarchs, but they still must conduct their business inside the organizational box, focused on the strategic mission. They may challenge conformity and attack cultural resistance, but they also know that their organization must be profitable to survive.

As a result, muralists must develop the endurance of a marathoner and the idealism of Quixote to be successful. And they need to continually remember what they learned off the beaten path that has given them the extra little wheels in their heads and in their hearts, and which gives them their passion and makes them "different."

So, do "nice guys" finish last? The bottomline is this. Don't mess with a muralist with a rack of antlers thinking they are just "nice" guys and easy prey unless you are prepared to meet their level of emotional intensity and personal commitment with a philosophy of your own, and a team behind you that is as equally passionate to succeed. After all, there is no second place in a cultural coup d'etat.

"You Don't Get To Be A Twelve-Point Muralist By Luck."

CHAPTER 18

The "Sport" Of Business

"In every organization, there are lifters and there are leaners, and there is a difference!"

If business was categorized as a competitive sport, the sport of business would be promoted as a classic matchup between two highly skilled, highly experienced, and highly competitive traditional rivals:

- Employees motivated by their self-interest to maximize earnings while minimizing effort.

vs.

- Managers motivated by their superiors to maximize performance while minimizing cost.

Unfortunately, in this "game" both sides lose if either side overwhelms the other. Organizations must make a profit, but their employees must also make a living. Without the appropriate and necessary level of tension (and mutual understanding) to maintain this often tenuous balance, either the costs will be too high or the output will be too low. Either way the organization will begin to disassemble.

The objective of mentor-leaders, therefore, must be to lead and educate, not to defeat and deflate their employees. If managers are going to be successful in the sport of business, they must know the "rules" and understand how the game is played. At the same time, however, they must also remain focused on the end game objective—sustaining a healthy and profitable organization—and not become distracted by the disabling tactics associated with winning at all costs. This means setting high expectations and rewarding the appropriate individuals for achieving them, (and exacting consequences on those who don't), while providing the leadership and strategic vision that enables both "sides" to win.

Extreme management styles do not typically work for long. Hard edged (not nice guy) managers who unyieldingly demand productivity without sufficient feedback and recognition will ultimately dispirit their people and send their organizations into a death spiral. "Nice guy" managers who fail to maintain the proper balance between enthusiasm and accountability will create more atmosphere than widgets.

In either case, "wheels" that are performance driven, but dispirited, or enthusiastic, but happily underperforming, produce the same result — organizational dysfunction. The only difference is that some employees know they are miserable, and others are just blissfully oblivious. The dynamics will only "make sense" to both groups when they are reunited in the unemployment line.

A Pack Of Luckies And A Country Song

I received a call at my home very late one night from a stressed out colleague in a hotel room half-way across the country. He had been threatened with the loss of his job if he failed to implement an aggressive, but less than specific plan of a "triple A" type manager—a monarch of the highest order. The project had kept him on the road for three months with no end in sight. I could tell from the time of his call and the pain in his voice that something was very wrong. In less than five minutes, I had heard about the complaints from his wife regarding his travel schedule, his guilt from missed soccer games and perhaps even worse, his overall doubt that what he was doing even mattered (why am I here?).

What emerged was the mental image of a defeated man, sitting in a far away hotel room, with a pack of Luckies and a bottle of bourbon on the night stand, a pistol on the bed, and a country song playing in the background. While this is certainly an exaggerated description, he definitely did not present the role of a happy camper or paint a healthy picture. It was obvious that he needed help.

After urging him to go home in the morning, and to take a week off to pull himself together, I related the story to the resident monarch. There was little compassion. He blamed the beleaguered employee for taking everything he had said about the implementation deadlines too literally. The manager was categorized as weak and not a "player," despite a positive reputation earned over 20 years. Nevertheless, the job was what it was, so the manager needed to do what was required, or be removed, either carrying his shield, or resting upon it.

While the employee ultimately recovered enough to retain his position and remain with the company, he was never the same again. His confidence was gone but he felt trapped by his twenty-two years of service with the company and pending college tuition bills. Two of his colleagues transferred out within a month of the event.

The project was subsequently dismantled within three years, under the next monarch's watch—but far too late for the manager who had already escaped to a lesser job in a different part of the organization.

Sadly, this is not an isolated event, nor is the following story, which once again shows that skills of managing and leading are often learned from unlikely sources. This one came from reading a good night story to my children when they were small.

The Message Of The Moose

"Thidwick the Good Hearted Moose" by Dr. Seuss is must reading for anyone needing to more clearly understand the delicate balance that exists in the sport of business. In the book, Thidwick is the "Mr. Nice Guy" manager who is so busy creating a cheery and sheltered environment for his expanding (but far too comfortable) "organization" of leaners (who nest in his antlers) that he completely neglects the essence of his responsibilities. When the leaners prove to be more successful game players, Thidwick misses a critical deadline for his personal survival because he has been considerably slowed down by his extra load.

Alas, Thidwick, the inefficient and "wannabe" lifter, has been dragged down by the leaners. In the sport of business, he is the big loser. This becomes very clear when the "firing squad" of hunters arrives. As usual, they are not looking for the "leaners" he has been coddling and nourishing. They rarely are. They are looking to shoot the one with the "antlers," friendly old Thidwick. The "protector" had become the prey.

This is not the way it is supposed to work, yet it happens all too often because managers do not sufficiently understand that ineffective leading, whether monarchic or muralistic, is not only harmful to their organizations— it can be fatal to them! In other words, no matter how you spin it, under whatever circumstances it happens, bad leading is bad leading.

The Moral—Lifters And Leaners, There Is A Difference!

Thankfully, fables have morals so Thidwick gets a second chance and we have the opportunity to learn from his mistakes. The loveable beast is ultimately spared when he has an eleventh hour epiphany (and a reprieve from Mother Nature). Few managers can rely on such good fortune in real life. Nevertheless, in just fifteen minutes of reading, this "children's" book provides a metaphorical reminder that when there are widgets to be made, the widgets must be made. When there are deadlines to be met, the deadlines must be met. And, in every organization, there are lifters, and there are leaners, and there is a difference!

The widget for managers is making certain that their employees are producing high caliber widgets, on time and on budget. This is pretty basic stuff, yet organizations are full of naïve managers with misplaced priorities like Thidwick. The only difference is that in the real world, the endings aren't usually quite as happy.

No wonder there is the perception that "nice guys finish last." However, it's usually not just that they're nice, it's also that they do not sufficiently understand the basic rules of the game. They fail to appreciate that in the "sport of business" there are natural tensions between the competeing parties that are as healthy as they are necessary. And, all participants must uphold their end of their responsibilities for the organization to succeed.

Contrary to what most employees might think, profitable survival is the primary objective of an organization. It's pretty basic. The "sport of business," therefore, is a precarious, yet critical, balancing act because neither "side" can afford to win completely, nor lose absolutely if the organization is to survive, let alone prosper. This is why good leaders are so valuable to organizations—they help both sides see the bigger picture and successfully guide the participants to effectively execute their roles and responsibilities within the rules of the game. The more effective the leaders, the less visible are their hands in the process.

For instance, monarchic managers who believe they can bully employees with daily doses of blunt trauma will get their reality check when their lifters leave and the wheels begin to fall off their organizations, or when they stumble into the wrong setting and discover a Pacman waiting in the weeds with a power pellet by his side and little remorse in his heart.

Conversely, the Thidwicks of the management world, who naively fail to understand that the personal objectives and motivations of the people they choose not to sufficiently challenge are contrary to both the organization's and their own survival needs, will continue to be perennial performance management targets. Some will think that they are being picked on because they are "nice guys." Others will blame their failures on bad luck. Both are wrong. It's about their failure to effectively perform within the rules of the "sport of business."

To be effective, therefore, muralists must understand that "daring to be different" is of little value if their energies are solely devoted to being daring, or being different. Their efforts are most valuable when they are directed to finding new answers to old questions, and playing to win within the rules of the "game." In fact, this is what makes muralists such effective leaders. By creating an environment in which employees are motivated to challenge their personal limits to be successful, they build a powerfully effective workforce that produces quality widgets. By working backwards from the end result (e.g., muralizing and kayaking), they create more efficient processes, faster project cycle times, lower cost, and a competitive advantage. In other words, muralists succeed when they "dare to be different" by addressing both sides of the sport of business equation.

Over time muralist leaders develop a culture in which high achievement is the expected norm, and poor performance is not tolerated. Lifters are rewarded; leaners are disappointed. And, here's a news flash—the employees know who among them are the lifters and leaners long before the managers find out. While few will advance the information, all are watching their managers and silently hoping that they will figure it out and fix it fast.

There are few words, and fewer tears when a leaner is discovered and removed. In fact, it validates the culture of high personal achievement. Besides, when leaners are excised from the operation, the only thing lost is their dead weight which is only slowing down the lifters.

It's the equivalent of modern day math, organizational style—addition by subtraction.

CHAPTER 19

Making Contact And Staying "In Touch"

"Muralists know that something magical is happening when they arrive early to turn on the lights, but the lifters have already beaten them to the switch."

Why do organizations appear to passively stand by and allow their best employees to "fire them" and leave for "better opportunities" in other companies, as if their terminations are more an inevitability of business than a failure of management?

Even when there is an eleventh-hour effort to salvage a valued, but terminating, employee with an offer of more money or the promise of a future promotion, the timing of the gesture is typically too late and usually fails. The official rationalization is that they just wanted to try different things or to move on to "greener pastures." The real reason for many employees, however, is that they wanted, or needed, to escape from under the control of stifling managers and hierarchic organizations, whose working environments provided more job-related anxiety and professional desperation, than a sense of achievement and personal inspiration.

When employees, particularly those with skill-related options valued in the employment market, are treated like resources and expected to mindlessly march in the parade, they tend to move from company to company until they find a more comfortable and personally satisfying employment fit. However, in organizations where leaders make their people feel positive about themselves and proud of their contributions, employees tend to be more committed to their careers and less likely to seek out, or be vulnerable to other proverbial opportunities or other companies.

This is so logical sounding that it can hardly be a secret, and must be included on the "Top Ten things a good manager must do" lists found in every management book out there. Yet, if it is true, then why do so many employees feel diminished by the lack of professional regard and personal respect for them from their managers?

Like my fraternity brother who had memorized all the steps for success for his big date, but who could not adapt or execute when it counted, many managers are chronically "unlucky" in this regard. They are so focused on their own goals and organizational mortality that they neglect to practice basic human-relation skills toward their employees that cost little in terms of time, and less in terms of expense, but yield incalculable benefit to their organizations.

As a result, they often end up being fired by their employees. The old commercial line of "pay me now or pay me later" clearly applies to managers who fail to make contact with their employees, and who are all thumbs when it comes to "the Feel."

The Handshake, With A Touch Of Humanity

One of the few mentor-leaders in my career once advised me to develop a good handshake and use it often. I watched the way he walked around his large operation, stopping at work areas along the way, shaking the hands of his employees as he went. Everyone delighted in his spontaneous visits. But, it was not just the handshake, it was the entire experience — the greeting, the laugh, a quick story, the word of encouragement, and the knowledge that he would be back.

When he moved on, he left smiling faces, and a touch of humanity in his wake. He knew every person's name and had a story about each one. He had "the Feel" for his organization because he was continually in touch with his people. Nobody ever "fired" him. To my regret, I have been associated with very few managers of his magnitude since, but I certainly learned a few things from him.

Promotions Are Less About You...And More About "Them"

For example, my first meeting with employees after I became a manager was a big disappointment. It was quite clear that they were not nearly as impressed by my promotion as I had been, so it's reasonable to conclude that my name had not yet made it onto my door. However, after a few days of thinking about what needed to be done, I remembered this mentor-leader and began walking around the office, stopping at each desk and shaking every hand. To my surprise, the employees hated it! I could actually hear the people talking about this unusual management behavior when they thought I was out of earshot. This was especially true for the women who particularly disliked the pain they felt when my hand pinched their rings against their fingers.

Nevertheless, I kept at it every day. However, not much changed until I began to better understand and focus on the key component of my new responsibilities—"them." What I had hoped would happen did not begin to occur until after I realized that my promotion was less about me and more about my better relating to and leading my employees. They were my "widget." What a revelation!

Once that happened I suddenly began to notice the pictures of their families and pets in their work areas, and I began to ask about them. They were very eager to talk about themselves and share their stories, even be addressed by their nicknames. The daily "handshake" soon became a highlight of their day, and a very critical part of mine. Over time, these daily visits helped reveal their hobbies and interests. Personalities emerged. There was laughter. Little by little I saw the people actually waiting for me to arrive at their desk by "warming up their handshake," like a pianist preparing to play. The women began removing their rings when they saw me in the area so they could give me a good one. The caliber of their handshakes and smiles improved. They even started greeting each other with a handshake each morning.

We were making contact, and as we did we began connecting, and the better that we connected, the better we communicated. Ideas for improving our operation began to emerge, most of them presented during the daily ritual while I was at their desk where they could show me what they had thought about and were doing, with several other employees gathered around and pitching in. Nobody had to come to my office to find me, because they knew that I would be looking for them, even if it was to just run through the office right before they left for the day.

Over the years, I have managed many groups in different departments and at various levels of organizations. Every person still gets a handshake and a few minutes every day when we can talk about what's happening in their lives or going on in their work. Some like it more than others, but nobody has ever said they didn't want the time or attention. In fact, most usually reach out their hand, smile, give me their best shake and occasionally say, "you're different."

The emotional connection can be overwhelming.

These are the bonds of mutual trust that form in muralistic teams that become the basis from which everything else develops. Everyone knows the plan and what is expected of them. There is a kayak and a paddle at every desk, and they know why they are there. They understand the deductive challenge of the "puzzle game," become skilled at visualizing the "Rorschach on the wall" and approach solutions from the back of the maze and work toward the front. In short, they get "*it*," and they deliver "*it*."

Muralists know that something magical is happening when they arrive early to turn on the lights, but the lifters have beaten them to the switch. Their "lights" are already turned on, and their wheels are in motion.

The Magic Words

However, a handshake, even a good one, has a distinct limitation—it must be done in person, an increasing difficulty in today's virtual business world. The challenge for leaders, therefore, is to perfect the fine art of the "verbal handshake." Muralists understand this well.

Employees love to see their names in print, especially when they are associated with a successful result. The positive impact of public recognition, in writing, is more powerful than most managers realize, and the cost is the same as a good handshake and longer lasting. If you think about it, it's probably the reason that some clever entrepreneur invented refrigerator magnets for proud parents to proudly display their child's latest success!

I have personally experienced the "overnight" cultural turnaround of an organization based primarily on the use of the magic words—the names of the employees—by publicly broadcasting their success stories (their "widgets"). However, like the handshake, publicizing positive performance was neither a cultural norm, nor an initial success. Many employees were content to hide their light under a bushel basket to avoid drawing attention to themselves. Some just wanted to be left alone to do their job and not be embarrassed by undue attention. Others just did not want to be "discovered."

While you might be able to appreciate the modesty, they were doing themselves and their organization a disservice. When value is not known, there is a perception, even a presumption, that there is no known value to what they do. When employee groups are perceived to have no value, they are the first ones to go when the order comes from the "ivory tower," hovering 30,000 feet above reality, to "bring expenses into line." This was a fate that had occurred four times in three years to this organization.

The employees in this department, once revered as the strongest corporate asset, had developed an operational inferiority complex. They behaved like grazing wildebeests waiting to be savaged by the next predator moving through their area with a mandate to pare back the herd. The immediate objectives were to revitalize their enthusiasm, restore their pride, and reestablish their value before they became an extinct organizational species.

The culture changed when their leader raised their bar, then publicized the value of their individual accomplishments to the organization every week. How coincidental! When the attitude of the leader changed, the attitude of the organization changed. It was amazing what happened when the wildebeests began to see their names in print—they began kicking up their heels and behaving like assets. More importantly, their tormentors also began regarding them as assets, not prey. In less than a year the predators turned to different targets who were easier to hunt and not moving as fast. It's funny how that works, isn't it?

What's The Story *You* Want To Tell?

By carefully selecting the stories for public recognition that demonstrate the desired and expected behavior of all employees, leaders send a series of very important signals to their organizations:

- Positive performances are important and valuable.
- The organization values positive performances.
- Your job is to produce positive performances.
- This is what a positive performance looks like, and
- The organization awaits your positive performance.

What happens to the organization is that natural competitive instincts emerge. When the first stories are published, the instinct of some employees is to top them with stories of their own. The culture suddenly demands that lifters emerge from their faceless anonymity to receive their recognition. The process snowballs until the nonparticipants either join the action or leave. Either is a positive result.

But it's not just publicizing the success stories that is important; it's about raising the bar, increasing expectations and changing organizational culture. Employees both gain status and begin feeling better about themselves when their colleagues begin to copy their best practices and to consult with them on similar problems.

Even more impactful, however, is the behavior of the leaders. Leaders must lead. Publicizing successes has positive value, but doing it only gets you part of the way there, unless the effort is sustained over enough time to get a critical mass of employees on board. It's amazing how quickly the word spreads about the leader's behavior. When the leader follows the story with an immediate call to provide a "verbal handshake" to the successful employee, the desired behavior is not just reinforced with the employee, but also with their colleagues. Recognition and attention become desirable. Everyone wants to be on the bus, especially when the bus is being driven by someone who knows where they are headed and is appreciative that you are aboard (and also has a roll of quarters in his pocket).

While there are endless ways to create the cultural verbal handshake, my own experience has shown that it takes fewer than ten minutes to create this environment. Here are four leading questions that can be asked when making your call to an employee to discuss their success:

1. How did you do it?
2. How did you feel when you were doing it?
3. What did the customer think about it?
4. What is your next story?

Employees want to have passion for their jobs and receive appreciation from their bosses for doing them well. They will talk as long as you will listen, so make the call. If you listen closely enough they will tell you more than you can imagine. Success follows success, and it all begins with a good handshake and the "magic words."

If you want to be a little more intimate, send a handwritten note to an employee who has been successful. You can limit the note to as few as three words and your signature as long as they say "good job" and "thanks." I guarantee that note will be on the refrigerator door by dinner time (but not before they think about how to get your next note).

Reading Your Mail, And Other Minimum Management Standards

However, when it comes to "staying in touch," we cannot ignore that much of today's communication is done by e-mail. In monarchic environments, e-mail is little more that the modern day remnant from Curley — a black hole. Messages from subordinates are often seemingly beneath the dignity of acknowledgment, let alone a response, from the boss. Of course, the lack of a response actually creates its own message which has unintended consequences for the monarch, since the speed of communication moves at the pace of the "leader." No wonder it always seems to be the "29th day" in monarchies.

Conversely, in muralistic cultures, e-mail is promptly acknowledged and personally answered by the muralist. However, in addition to e-mail, reports are read and meaningful feedback is immediately and constructively provided. Positive points are acknowledged. Assumptions are challenged. Thought provoking questions are raised. Wisdom and enthusiasm intersect. Quality standards are expanded. Because the trust level is high in muralistic cultures, the report is often circulated for additional, and helpful, feedback from fellow team members, who better understand the interconnections of their respective wheels as a result.

By behaving like a leader, you challenge your people to become lifters by helping them rise to higher levels of personal accomplishment. This is how you become a mentor-leader.

Many employees have been quietly waiting their entire careers for this very moment.

The process is symbolic of the culture—fast and efficient, open and honest, involved and evolving, positive and uplifting. Who wants to be the person sending even ordinary work to a muralist who actually reads their mail in a timely manner and who willingly gets into your kayak, and helps you navigate to a successful result?

The result is that muralists-in-training feel good about themselves and their work, because their leader is holding up their performance to the organizational mirror.

They like their reflection.

CHAPTER 20

The Leadership Compass

"Within the realm of life's opportunities, you are either on the field and in the game or at the game but in the stands. If you play it safe, grandstand bound, you'll be just another nobody not in the game."

What happens in organizations where the leaders do not sufficiently understand the sport of business or the law of the schoolyard; or fail to recognize the difference between their lifters and leaners; or seem to be chronically mired in the 29th day of their business issues?

They have recurring "Yogi Berra" management moments!

Picture the scenario. The manager is frantically looking over an office of cubicles occupied by employees, many of whom have been with the organization for years. There are high-profile projects to be managed and a promotion to be made. Immediate solutions to pending issues must be found. However, the answers to these organizational needs do not instantly appear from among the people in the cubicles. The manager turns to the Human Resource Director and says, "Call the head hunter. We've got some big jobs to fill, but nobody works here anymore."

The HR person will dutifully do their job, but in the process they will create at least three other problems for the organization:

1. Dispirit the apparent "nobody's" in the cubicles who had aspirations of moving up in the organization (but who were unaware that they were considered a "nobody").

2. Anger the existing managers and project leaders when the higher price tags for the newly recruited somebody's are discovered.
3. Entrust important projects to managers new to the organization whose failure to deliver will not be realized until after additional capable employees have left for lack of opportunity.

Performance Issue Or Management Problem?

If the HR person was really doing their job, they would interrupt the discussion and ask, "Does our organization have a performance problem or a leadership problem?" The odds are excellent that it is the latter, and the chances are also very good that "Yogi the Manager" has never coached a youth football team, nor understands the need to get his players into the game.

With all that is written about Human Resource Development, not to mention the annual cost of HRD, why are organizations so chronically ineffective at handling and developing their personnel? Why is there a persistent feeling that somebody new from somewhere else, who knows little about the organization and less about its culture and challenges, has more talent or is better suited to lead than the person already in the building? (Conversely, why is it that other companies are able to see the unrecognized talent and untapped potential of your employees who unremorsefully fire you to accept higher level opportunities elsewhere)?

Part of the explanation rests within the very pool of people who "hope" for a promotion, yet who never quite dare enough to be different or sufficiently demonstrate their readiness or even the potential to lead. They are the life forms in the daily parade, who show little spark and even less enthusiasm, except when programmatically marching past the judges, or at review time. They misguidedly believe that having a clean uniform and keeping in step over the course of the march—or even just "working hard"—are the prime prerequisites for promotion.

However, in maintaining such a low profile, they have also missed the critical point. Within the realm of life's opportunities, you are either on the field and in the game, or at the game but in the stands. No matter how you cut it, a leaner is still a leaner, and leaners should never be confused with lifters. If you play it safe, grandstand bound, you'll be just another nobody not in the game.

The other side of the equation, therefore, is how organizations recognize and evaluate their talented employees; how they challenge them to excel; how they encourage their lifters to stay and create the urgent need for their leaners to leave; and how they prepare and develop their most talented assets for increased responsibility—then make it happen.

These functions often tend to fall within the annual performance review process. For the most part, personnel evaluation procedures are only questionably effective. Actually, without a proactive plan the process can be dispiriting, especially to better employees.

Performance Reviews And Other Riddles...

Consider this partial mix of objectives and messages involved in the evaluation process:

- Compare actual results with objectives and expectations
- Recognize successes and accomplishments
- Discuss/address performance deficits
- Rationalize salary increases
- Raise the performance bar
- Listen
- Motivate
- Review the employee's value to the organization
- Place employees in rank order of performance
- Produce a promotion list
- Present a career development plan
- Evaluate the manager's ability to oversee/evaluate their employees

Ideally, personnel development, counseling, and communication routinely occur throughout the year, covering all of these points (and others) at various times along the way. This is especially critical in providing the appropriate challenges, direction and compensation to employees with leadership potential.

However, with the increased spans of control for managers, not to mention the expanding distances separating them from their direct reports, (superimposed on the rigors of their own operational responsibilities), this important dialogue typically takes place as little as is required, and often by telephone. Worse, emerging leaders may be missed because they either get lost or do not get enough "looks" to be seen.

When these important interactions are limited, an interesting personnel paradox emerges. The expectations of employees at "review time" are enlarged because performance evaluations are typically an annual event, and there is something of measurable and lasting personal, professional, and financial value at stake. At the same time, however, the event is diminished because there is a feeling, often accurate, that the manager does not know them well enough to complete an accurate or fair evaluation, or that they have not invested sufficient time and effort to do them justice.

Consequently, the review meeting often becomes more emotional than objective because the employees usually do not know what to expect entering the process, or how well they are valued, until they formally see it in front of them.

The employees are understandably focused on receiving written acknowledgment of, and recognition for their successes, along with increased compensation, and a discussion of future promotional opportunities. However, the process often reduces their ongoing contributions, and even their victories, to a brief dialogue about their satisfactory delivery of results for which they had been paid to produce (e.g., for doing their job), before "zeroing in" on their perceived areas for improvement.

As a result, the discussion typically produces more critical feedback than anticipated by the employee, and overemphasizes negatives that they are often hearing for the first time. Consequently, it is not atypical for employees to emerge from their meetings feeling more despaired than inspired.

My Boss Doesn't Understand Me...
And Other Truths

What further complicates the process is that the manager is often faced with the challenging task of preparing multi-paged forms with numerous micro measures that overly scrutinize an employee's abilities and results, from the top priority objectives to the most minute activity. It is often very difficult for even those managers who have placed the appropriate time and thought into this process to fully report on each phase of the employee's responsibilities, because they are often not familiar enough with their work to intelligibly comment. Consequently, the review can become anecdotal and personality based.

No wonder employees often feel emotionally trapped by their jobs. They often enter a personnel process unsure of the outcome, and receive a report which is often too superficial to sufficiently distinguish a lifter from a leaner. This is particularly true when the process forces performance ratings to numerically balance to an organizational "average" (suggesting that performance recognition is measured against the mythical average person). This is especially defeating for lifters whose accomplishments may be diminshed to statistically accommodate less productive performers.

Not surprisingly, many lifters leave the evaluation process feeling undervalued, and that their manager has too little understanding, and less appreciation, of what they do or how well they do it. The result is predictable. The lifters look for an escape route and leave, and the leaners stay—just the reverse of what the organization needs.

No wonder "nobody" works there anymore!

Protect Your Winners

How do muralists avoid this situation by retaining their better employees and creating a winning environment?

Here's a basic fact: an organization cannot move forward when its best employees are leaving and its marginal employees remain to assume the important leadership roles by default. What quickly evolves is a "culture of the mediocracy," which devolves with each passing business generation.

The **Leadership Compass** that follows (see Figure 20.1) is a model that I have personally used for over twenty years and is a model of how muralists can manage their organizations by better evaluating their assets and communicating their findings based on four overarching components of performance: skills, effort, attitude and results.

The Leadership Compass provides an ongoing performance evaluation tool and a road map for both the manager and the managed. Its objective is to tailor the appropriate development plan to the individual's talents and contributions for optimum "wheel" utilization within the organizational strategy.

The key to the "compass" is direct and honest communication, since the process is completely interactive. Both the manager and the employee make commitments to one another which directly lead to either enhanced performance or exit from the organization. Therefore, the manager must have more than a passing familiarity with the employee and their work product. And, the employee must understand how effectively their work fits within the organizational strategy.

Let The Lifting (Or Leaning) Begin...

Unlike the failed youth football coach, this process requires that the manager provide each employee the equivalent of a helmet, a ball, an opportunity—and a push in the right direction with training, coaching, and ongoing support.

However, equality of opportunity is not to be confused with equality of result. When the whistle blows and the game begins, it's up to the employees to pull their weight and get it done.

Let the lifting—or leaning—begin.

It is important, therefore, to view the Leadership Compass as a highly dynamic and reiterative process because employees continually transition between performance quadrants as their jobs change and their experience levels increase. The actual process is very easy, although not especially "simple." It requires an understanding of the key issues prior to the meeting, responsive listening while it is underway, agreement on a plan when the meeting concludes, and follow-up action through the year.

The objective is to lead (not defeat) employees by clearly communicating their organizational roles and performance expectations while reviewing their results within them. Therefore, since the process involves asset development, the meeting environment should always be constructive, not confrontational.

FIGURE 20.1   The Leadership Compass

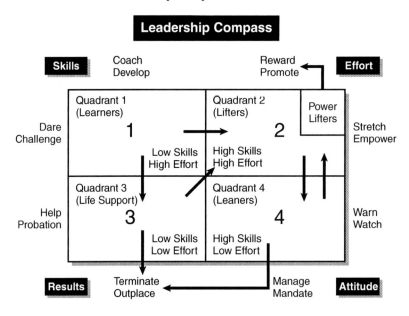

Prior to the meeting, both the employee and the manager separately assess the critical job components on a performance scale (e.g., what is being measured), and identify the employee's appropriate placement in the leadership compass. The more relevant examples that can be presented as supportive "proof points," the better.

The resulting dialogue regarding performance levels on critical job objectives and results, and quadrant placement removes the mystery about where the employee "is," how they are valued, and how they can improve, because it's all right there on the Compass, mapped in front of them.

The concept works because wherever the employee fits in the Leadership Compass, a strategic and personalized plan is developed that is clear and useful for both the manager and the employee. It provides direction to both since they must work together over time for the employee to reach the next level of asset development, and personal achievement.

Quadrant 1—High Effort, Low Skills (The Learners)

All employees begin in Quadrant 1. This is the "learning" phase of the process and applies equally to newly hired and newly promoted employees as they learn their jobs. The objective for managers of learners is to provide the appropriate level of orientation to the organization, and the training, information, and personalized direction to help them begin their new responsibilities and become productive.

This group of employees is enjoyable to manage. They characteristically have an excellent attitude and are eager to learn their new jobs and to progress in their careers. The immediate responsibility of the manager, therefore, is to leverage their enthusiasm by patiently coaching them to quickly increase their knowledge and build their confidence. As the learners begin to grasp their roles, the emphasis turns to challenging them with more advanced assignments, daring them to more independently apply their learning, and expecting them to become increasingly successful in situations where failure is a distinct possibility.

As soon as appropriate to the individual, managers must evaluate the potential of their learners to be productive assets and move them along to the next stage of their progression. If the employee selection process has been effective, most new employees move to Quadrant 2.

Quadrant 2—High Effort, High Skills (The Lifters)

If Quadrant 1 is the investment phase, Quadrant 2 is the pay-off place where the most productive organizational assets exist. This is where the lifters are located. These employees represent the backbone of the organization due to their expanding skill levels, high energy, and conscious competence. In terms of the story, the strategy and the widget, they "get it," and they can produce it profitably. Their results carry the organization.

The more advanced, although not necessarily the more tenured, employees (better known as "power lifters") simultaneously demonstrate their ability to work from the back of the maze, to become "Rorschach on the wall" muralizers, and to consistently deliver a quality product on time and on budget. Everybody knows who these people are because not only do they have "the Look," they also have the best results.

While these employees are also a joy to manage due to their positive attitudes and ability to deliver results, they also present an interesting (but significant) leadership challenge. At some point, everyone in Quadrant 2 comes to a personal crossroads between conscious competence and conscious complacence. Muralists understand that lifters, particularly the "power lifters," are both very precious and very fragile because they are so emotionally connected to their work. For this reason they are constantly finding opportunities to stretch their lifters' limits, to empower them with greater responsibilities, to reward their contributions, and to promote them to areas of greater responsibility.

Quadrant 3—Low Effort, Low Skills
(Life Support)

Though all employees are hired with the anticipation of success, some will not measure up to those expectations. Consequently, new employees must be slotted into Quadrant 3 for organizational "life support" when they have not shown the ability or the aptitude to assimilate into the organization or to successfully adapt to their new responsibilities during the learning phase.

Some employees are just slow to adapt and need additional training or more individualized attention. If they can be resuscitated early enough (i.e. provided "life support"), many are soon redirected and on their way to becoming productive employees.

However, as hard as you might try to rehabilitate them, others simply just do not successfully "get it." In these cases, after the appropriate measures have been tried and failed, termination and outplacement are the necessary strategies. The sooner this is completed, the better. Time spent with those on "life support" who are unlikely to become lifters in a reasonable time frame adds negative value, wastes time and money, and, (more significantly) delays investment in more qualified candidates.

Quadrant 4—Low Effort, High Skills
(The Leaners)

Quadrant 4 is the real scourge of organizations because it is the place where the leaners lurk. These are the people who at some point in their careers were seen as organizational up and comers. They have the skills and ability to do their jobs, but do not consistently exercise sufficient effort or positive attitude to do them. Over time they have been allowed to become professionally dispirited, comfortably complacent, and decreasingly relevant. They must be constantly watched, warned, and reminded of their deliverables and deadlines. For a group that should produce significant results, and need little direction in the process, they consistently underproduce, and require a significant amount of managing, monitoring, and mandating for their "effort."

This is not to confuse leaners with the "life support" group in Quadrant 3. In many ways, leaners are the direct by-product of management's inability to sufficiently stretch, empower, and reward employees who were once considered to be lifters. Over time they have become the personification of management's failure to develop and promote the talented or eliminate the untalented.

Leaners do not inspire others to develop or display positive attitudes. They passively discourage excellence. Worse, as managers, they block places in the organization (and often for years) which would be better staffed by up and coming lifters, many of whom will ultimately leave for lack of encouragement or opportunity. Therefore, people in Quadrant 4 must be either "rediscovered" or rooted out—and as soon as possible—before they damage the organization.

The message to managers of leaners is to show them where they fit in the leadership compass, and either help them to help themselves back into Quadrant 2 to resume lifting their load, or encourage them to leave the organization.

This requires the manager to review and re-evaluate a leaner's skills, and to "give them a hill"—a specific and meaningfully important challenge with a deadline—that leverages their experience, stretches their abilities, and helps them rediscover the passion, pride, and relevance that they had demonstrated when they were working their way up in the organization and earning their "points."

By challenging the leaners to get back into the game with a high-profile project, their die is cast. The manager will either rediscover that "that nobody" in the cubicle is really a "somebody" badly in need of a new challenge (and better leading), and ready to get back into the play, or the employee will conclusively understand that they have in fact become just another nobody not in the game.

If You Don't Think That Lifters Are Rare, Try To Replace One...

The keys to your organization are readily apparent. It's about talent! The process begins with an understanding of the organization's story, and expands to recruiting and retaining the best employees who can learn it, believe it, tell it, and deliver it.

The organization's "lifters" are critical. They are the backbone of the organization due to their conscious competence and ability to produce quality widgets. They attract other lifters. They create a competitive advantage. They are the next generation of leaders who understand how effective organizations work and the ones who are ready to develop their own employees in the same fashion.

However, if their skills and profit-yielding potential are obvious to you, they are no less obvious to other organizations. The strategy to retain lifters should be as clear as the tactics to redirect leaners. Therefore, organizations must compete for them, even in the absence of formalized "competition," to sustain their employment before an actual competitor makes you compete to retain them in real time. By then, it is often too late.

Keep in mind that competing is not solely about compensation. That's only one side of the sport of business equation. The other side is leading. If you want good people, have good leaders.

Had our "Yogi the Manager" known how to better identify and retain his lifters, he would not be in quite the predicament he is now, as he looks over the sea of cubicles filled with "nobody's."

The most significant problem for his organization, however, is probably not that "nobody" works there any more. It's that *nobody* has been leading them all along.

It's funny how that works.

CHAPTER 21

The Performance Index

"It isn't easy, and it isn't always 'nice.' However, it's also never about luck. That's why they call it leading, and that's how leaders earn their points."

Despite an expectation that they will lead, most managers feel powerless to act outside the comfort zone of the cultural norm. Many managers are simply incapable of changing anything of significance in their organizations without receiving a formal "order" to do it. This allows them to blame superiors for actions they must take, and frees them from the burden of self initiative and personal risk ("don't blame me..."). Perhaps this is why the term "good leader" has become almost an oxymoron. After all, cultural barriers and paper handcuffs are hard to break, even for a manager with a hacksaw. Therefore, while it's helpful to have tools like the Leadership Compass and theories about lifters and leaners, they are of little value in the hands of managers who can repeat the words but do not know how to put them into action.

For instance, personnel evaluation tools, including the Leadership Compass, provide the means to assess performance and tailor development plans on an individual basis. While this is important and necessary, how do managers assess the overall effectiveness of their entire organization—a much more important, yet seldom required measurement?

Muralistic leaders transcend organizational inhibitors by using the right tool at the right time to achieve exceptional results, even if they have to creatively develop a new application. Once again, the sources of discovery aren't always "conventional."

It's All In The Translation...

Several years ago I was running a training session for a group of new managers, one of whom had the sudden urge to ask an oddly timed, yet unforgettable, question, "What was the most important subject that [I] had ever studied?"

Trying my best not to renege upon the oft repeated, but seldom believed, "There's no such thing as a stupid question" pledge that every trainer feels obliged to advocate, my mind raced for an appropriate response. After a brief second, I blurted out my answer, "Latin."

The roomful of trainees began to chuckle, as though my answer was dumber than the question that had preceded it. Mercifully one kind soul bailed me out by asking for an explanation.

I responded by telling the group that I had taken Latin for six years at the Boston Latin School, where traditions as the oldest public school in America date back to 1635. Every night for homework I had to study lengthy Latin passages from Caesar, Cicero, Homer, and Virgil; then translate and recite them in class the following day under the harsh scrutiny of the "Master," to whom Latin was as alive and well as when Caesar was perfecting the art of arrogance, and Cicero was still in the oratory business. It was an intimidatingly difficult and time-consuming course of study. In fact, most students couldn't keep up, fell behind, and soon transferred to other schools.

However, this rigorous training helped develop a few very valuable management skills:

• The ability to translate abstract language into understandable English
• The mental discipline to do it quickly and often
• The capacity to report results under the pressure of a deadline, and
• The concept of daily accountability.

What was the difference, I suggested, between a page filled only with Latin words, or a page containing only numbers? It's all in the translation!

How do muralists translate their abstract data into actionable information and subsequent results? How do they enhance overall performance by better understanding how their individual parts (their human assets) most effectively fit into the organizational whole? How do muralists know what they need to do to be more effective leaders?

The Leadership Compass provides the tool to help make this happen.

Leadership Compass Case Study

For instance, consider the case of a manager in a moderately entrepreneurial organization who uses the Leadership Compass, and sets the following effectiveness benchmarks for its personnel in each of the four quadrants in Figure 21.1:

- Learners - 20%
- Lifters - 65% (20% of whom are "Power Lifters")
- Leaners - 5%
- Life Support - 10%

FIGURE 21.1 The Model for Organizational Performance

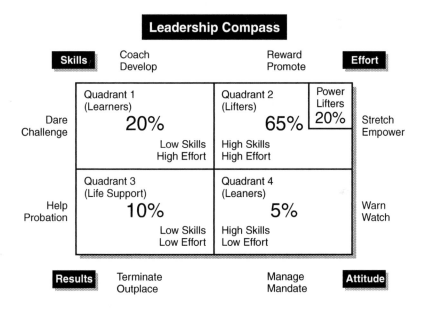

In this example, Lifters (Q2) have an organizational value of 1.0 (e.g. 100% effective). However, the value of employees assigned to both the Learner (Q1) and Leaner (Q4) Quadrants, in this model, is only .8 (80% effective):

- The Learners group cannot—by definition—perform up to 100% of expectation while they are learning their new jobs.
- Leaners do not—by definition—consistently perform up to 100% of their capabilities.
- There is no value for employees on Life Support (Q3).

Managers can use this tool as aggressively as their organizations demand or their needs require. For example, Q1 Learners could be assigned a value of .5 (50% effective), or, the desired percentage of Q2 Lifters could be 70% or "power lifters" could be assigned a value of 1.1 (110% effective) etc. The keys are to adapt the tool to fit organizational needs and to use consistent values over time to measure and compare progress.

Let's assume that after an appropriate opportunity for evaluation, the *actual* performance of the organization is shown in Figure 21.2.

FIGURE 21.2   Actual State of Performance

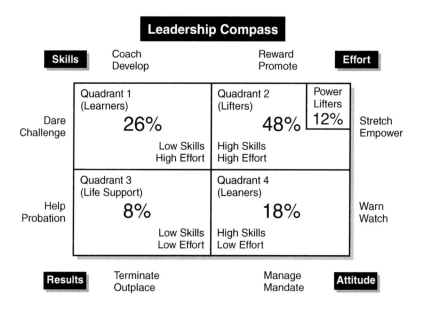

The next step, and critical challenge, is to translate these data into an organizational plan of action to improve the overall performance by comparing the actual result with the model benchmark.

The Numbers Can Speak...

Here's how to translate the Leadership Compass into "organizational English."

Figures 21.1 and 21.2 show us that we can calculate a mathematically-based Performance Index when the strategic values (e.g., the organizational components that comprise acceptable performance standards relating to skills, effort, attitude, and results) are established and compared—the actual to the benchmark:

Benchmark Performance Index

In Figure 21.1, the model benchmark organizational Standard of Performance (SP) is the following:

$$[\text{Sum} (.8 \times Q1) + Q2] \times [\text{Sum } Q2 + (.8 \times Q4)] = SP$$
$$[(.8 \times .20) + .65] \times [.65 + (.8 \times .05)] = SP$$
$$(.81) \times (.69)$$
$$.559 = \text{Benchmark Organizational Standard of Performance}$$

Actual Performance Index

The actual organizational Standard of Performance, represented by Figure 21.2, is lower than optimum:

$$[\text{Sum} (.8 \times Q1) + Q2] \times [\text{Sum } Q2 + (.8 \times Q4)] = SP$$
$$[(.8 \times .26) + .48)] \times [.48 + (.8 \times .18)]$$
$$(.69) \times (.62) = SP$$
$$.428 = \text{Actual Standard of Performance}$$

Therefore, this organization is performing at the following "Performance Index":

$$\text{Actual Performance} / \text{Standard of Performance} = PI$$
$$(.428 / .559) = PI$$
$$77\% = \text{Performance Index}$$

Commencement

The manager now knows that the organization is performing at a "C+" level, creating significant room for improvement. However, like commencement, the translation of these data marks only the beginning of the process. The next step, therefore, is the critical one—converting the data into the actionable information that leads to improved results.

For instance, Figure 21.3 demonstrates part of the problem this organization is facing—only 66% of its assets are performing with a skill level sufficiently high enough to meet the organization's needs. Without additional skill development, successful achievement of the organizational objectives is virtually impossible.

FIGURE 21.3   Skill Level

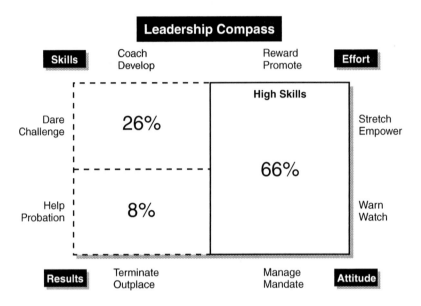

Consequently, some of the possible areas for translation from the manager's investigation might be the following:

- Are the most appropriate people being hired into the organization? (Relates to hiring practices and employee profiles.)
- Are the Lifters "firing" the organization, leaving the Leaners to run the business? (Relates to career development and compensation practices.)
- Are the training programs currently in place sufficient to meet the needs and demands of employees engaged in the real world? (Relates to training and development practices.)
- Are managers recognizing their potentially talented performers early enough in the Learner Phase, then daring, challenging, coaching, developing, and empowering them to become Lifters? (Relates to organizational management.)
- Is the organizational vision clear enough, the mission perceived worthy enough, and the managers seen as good enough by the lifters to remain in the organization? (Relates to the Don Quixote concept.)

In addition, Figure 21.4 shows that the manager's new organization needs an energy boost. Only 74% of the employees are viewed as exhibiting sufficient effort to consistently perform their responsibilities.

A similar evaluation is needed to better understand the "why and the because" of this organizational anemia, then to change the equation with the same courage, curiosity, and conviction of the managing monk, the irrepressible gymnast, and the child with the starfish.

FIGURE 21.4   Effort Level

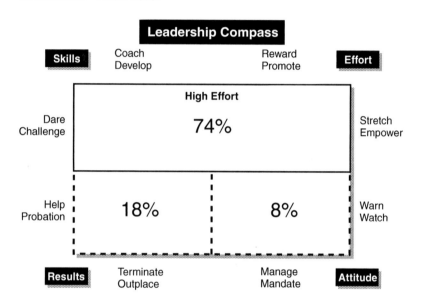

An evaluation might reveal:

- Monarchic managers are routinely dispiriting up-and-coming employees.
- There is little or no positive feedback between managers and employees regarding their work (e.g., Curley example).
- The pay/reward differential between lifters and leaners is too small, creating a cult of the mediocrity.
- Opportunities for lifters are being blocked by leaners.
- There is poor communication of the organizational vision.
- The organization's leaders are the wrong behavioral models.

The list of issues is virtually endless, but once the performance gaps have been translated into the organization's business language the leadership challenge and actionable options become clearer. The real questions are whether or not the current group of managers are capable of changing behavior and executing a better plan, or if the organization is prepared to find different leaders who will.

The objective of the Leadership Compass, therefore, is to help leaders maximize performance by recognizing both organizational and individual strengths and weaknesses, then creating the appropriate courses of improvement to change the dynamics and improve the results.

It isn't easy, and it isn't always "nice." However, it's also never about luck. That's why they call it leading, and that's how leaders earn their points.

CHAPTER 22

The Relevant Leader

"[Leading] ultimately comes down to a manager's ability to think and act and be a leader. The good news is that the timing couldn't be any better. When managers are ready to lead, their people are usually equally ready to follow."

I enjoy managing, but what I really like most is leading. I also enjoy discussing the essence of being a leader. But, like most things, enough is enough, something I learned one night at a retirement party.

The hall was filled with the friends and colleagues of a very popular and highly respected manager. Seated at the head table in the front of the room were five speakers, all waiting to pay homage to, and fire their last shots at, their esteemed colleague. When the festivities began to run late, the emcee passed the word down the table asking the roasters to limit their comments to three minutes.

Everyone complied until the final speaker. Five minutes into his spiel, the emcee began pointing at his watch, but the gesture was ignored. Five minutes later, the long-winded raconteur was still so busy insulting guests in the audience that he had not yet even acknowledged the retiree. The emcee grabbed at his pant leg to get his attention, but his hand was abruptly swatted away.

Hit Me Again, I Can Still Hear Him!

When five more minutes passed with no end in sight, the emcee had heard enough. Summoning all his nerve, he lunged from his seat intending to smash the spielster in the mouth. Unfortunately, he telegraphed his move and the speaker ducked under his punch. Instead the blow landed squarely on the jaw of the startled retiree, knocking him backwards, out of his chair and off the platform. The audience gasped in horror, even as the speaker droned on, oblivious to the commotion that he had caused behind him.

When the embarrassed emcee finally reached the honoree, he frantically pleaded, "Are you OK?" The dazed retiree looked up at him, sighed and said, "No, hit me again, I can still hear him."

Taking that as a clue, it's time to put all of this into a final perspective of what it means to be a relevant leader.

Monarchic Control Versus Muralistic Leading

This book makes a clear distinction between monarchs and muralists and their organizational relevance, particularly relating to the distinction between managing and leading. While both responsibilities are significant pieces of the job, the leadership component has been the primary focus. Consequently, many facets of managing have not been discussed at length. For instance, in all organizations there are (nonhuman) resources and budgets that must be managed. There are numerous daily management decisions that must be made regarding relationships with customers and suppliers, establishing priorities, setting production schedules, and meeting other deadlines. There are also a multitude of human resource issues and organizational rules and procedures to be addressed in the traditional and formalized sense of managing.

While important and necessary, achieving proficiency in these tasks and functions does not create leaders. They are not the skills or values which inspire employees to achieve higher levels of success, or dare them to be different, or reach for even a single star. However, procedural controls, and the hierarchical structures in which they operate, do sustain monarchs, one of whom in my experience proudly boasted, "They call me the taskmaster and I welcome the title." (We had a different name for him that he would have found far less thrilling).

Therefore, while management positions traditionally include a multitude of tasks, many of which can consume significant time, the "leading" piece remains a paradox to most managers. They see the "bold colors" that other managers see clearly enough, but most cannot visualize the subtle tones that leaders feel. This makes it easier to understand why so many managers fail to become leaders. Somebody forgot to tell the employees that their manager was also supposed to be their "leader," and nobody told the managers that they were supposed to behave like one.

Muralist Or Monarch Or "Muralarch"?

I wonder how long it took to discover that combining black and white created gray, "the official color of business." The problem about "gray," however, is that there are so many variations that finding the right tone is often difficult. The more black in the blend, the darker the shade; the more white in the mix, the lighter the gray.

The same concept applies to the leadership styles of monarchs and muralists. Few, if any, leaders are monochromatic. Therefore, despite their different approaches, monarchs and muralists must constantly listen to each another and even occasionally acknowledge that the other side has an important point or the more relevant position. Over time, compromises are necessary as both sides compete for the cultural high ground by smoothing out the sharper edges of philosophies which may be too vague to attract followers, or too extreme to gain organizational support.

Their "tone," therefore, is a reflection of both their passion for their position and their willingness to compromise. The darker their shade, the more dogmatic the monarch; the lighter the gray, the more devoted the muralist.

Leadership Continuum

The issue for managers, therefore, is their placement on the "gray scale." The following Leadership Continuum (see Figure 22.1) provides an opportunity to evaluate your leadership style. You will need to self-assess your attitudes and feelings regarding sixty leadership characteristics, record your responses, and calculate the average to find your place. If you want additional objectivity (and a more valuable "awareness" experience), complete the exercise with colleagues, or your staff, and compare notes.

While the exercise is not scientific, you should find it interesting, thought-provoking, and hopefully insightful (especially if you do it with a colleague). For example, in the comparison of the leadership characteristics "attract new talent" versus "repel the talented," assess whether strong performers are routinely seeking to become associated with you, or if your talented people consistently find reasons to leave your organization. If you are a virtual magnet for talent, score yourself a 1 or 2; if you are a talent repellent, score a 6 or 7 depending on the level of your magnetism or degree of repulsion. If your results are mixed, score yourself accordingly.

FIGURE 22.1

Leadership Continuum

Muralist						Monarch
1	2	3	◁ 4	5	6	7

Leadership Characteristics — Score (Column 1)

Characteristic	Score	Opposite
See around corners		Constantly behind the curve
Contagious energy		Infectious lethargy
Instinctively evolving		Extinctively devolving
Give credit		Want credit
Run up the down escalator		Take the elevator one floor at a time
Dream in color		Sleep without dreaming
Paddle forward looking ahead		Row forward looking backward
Today's my day		Today's the 29th day
Hard nosed		Hard headed
Exercise enthusiasm		Exorcise enthusiasm
Go for it		Wait for it
Serve employees		Served by employees
Pick up starfish		Pass out bad habits
Always out front		Always "stuck in the middle"
Mentor		Manipulator
"You're different"		One size fits all
In the know		In the no
Free think		Echospeak
Wheel that works		Spinning wheel
Clear communication		Indecipherable "messages"
Always have a plan		Always have a problem
Think execution		Need execution
See the "Rorschach on the wall"		Need to receive "the memo" first
Learn from children		Treat employees like children
Make everyone a part		Take everyone apart
Do what's needed		Do what's required
Think and do		Obey
Consciously competent		Consciously complacent
Have "the Look"		Look for excuses
Organization moving in sync		Organization headed down the drain
Column 1 Subtotal		

Leadership Characteristics — Score (Column 2)

Characteristic	Score	Opposite
Commit to doing their best		Commit to trying their best
On the field, in the game		At the game, in the stands
In motion		Inaction
Inspire respect		Demand respect
Viewed as a hero		Seen as a victim
Enjoyable days		Happy daze
Create new ideas		Always "the devil's advocate"
Attract new talent		Repel the talented
Trust creation		Ass covering
Feel the subtle tones		See only the bold colors
Promote their philosophy		Protect their power
Break their paper handcuffs		Prisoner of the past
Consistently lucky		Chronically unlucky
Ready, aim, fire		Ready, aim, aim . . .
Build up the positives		Play up the negatives
Great for their ego		Grate on their ego
Motivated by ambitions		Paralyzed by inhibitions
Ain't no mountain high enough		Make mountains out of molehills
How can we fix it?		Who's to blame?
Name is on the door		Revolving doors
Soar over a higher bar		Limbo under a higher bar
Cluttered desk/clear mind		Clear desk/cluttered mind
Miles to go before I sleep		Asleep at the switch
Long leash and a rapid pace		Choker collar to control the pace
Out of the foxhole, "follow me"		Hunker down, "wait and see"
On the wave		On the beach
The answers are different		The answers remain the same
Lifter		Leaner
Leader		Manager
Twelve point buck		Twelve point mule
Column 2 Subtotal		

$$\frac{\text{Column 1} + \text{Column 2}}{60} = \text{Average Leadership Score}$$

Scores that average from 3.0–5.0 suggest that you are a hybrid manager ("muralarch"). While it is a plus that you have an open mind and can make compromises, it's also likely that you don't have a distinct leadership philosophy either. You probably tend to go along to get along and hope for the best. If you want to "escape," you will need to take more personal risk to break out of your box, or spend the rest of your workdays defensively rationalizing why you always seem to be stuck "in the middle."

Scores averaging above 5.0 increasingly show monarchic leanings. You like process, procedure, power, and knowing that everything and everybody are where they should be—queued up and awaiting your approval. You value loyalty, formality, and tradition. All roads lead to you, and while you "have friends who are muralists," you wouldn't be entirely sad if a few of them got lost and couldn't find their way back while they were doing their off the beaten path thing.

Averages below 3.0 suggest that you are already on your way to transitioning from manager to muralistic leader. You offer alternative points of view, accept the risks associated with startup operations or undertaking projects that are on the organizational respirator, and take great pleasure in finding the right team to bring them to life. You question conventional wisdom and seek out new answers to old questions, even when not asked. Others see you as "different" (and tell you). The closer you are to 3.0, the more likely that you are still looking for the right muralist with whom to associate; the closer to 1.0, the more likely that you are the person they are seeking.

If Leading Were Easy, More Would Just Do It And Fewer Would Write About It...

Leading is not easy. If it were, more people would do it well and fewer would write about it. Unfortunately, managers cannot find all their "how to be a leader" answers in books. Perhaps part of the reason for this is that there are so many theories of leadership out there that the more you read, the greater the opportunity for confusion. Besides, how many managers can really relate to the larger than normal life roles, responsibilities, and experiences of military and sports figures often cited as leadership models?

Even if the books were clearer, the blunt reality is that the real world for most managers is far less dramatic and much more mundane than the world of the "hero." Their principal concerns are less about hand-to-hand combat or winning the World Series, and more about managing through unclear objectives and day-to-day survival. However, they tend to forget, or never quite understand, that "their" widget is ensuring that their employees are capable of producing *their* widget. Consequently, while many managers might desire to be viewed as leaders, most fail to move to the higher level of mentor-leader because they become neither a mentor, nor a leader.

In the end, too many managers rationalize that it's just easier to take the familiar path of least resistance and mindless (but presumably acceptable) mediocrity, and practice the practices that have been practiced on them in the past. They conform to the norm and they have the paper handcuffs and flat heads to prove it. Unless they escape from the parade, they become less and less relevant until they become redundant managers who need either a new "hill" to re-energize their enthusiasm and regain their under-utilized skills, or separation from the organization.

Perhaps the simple answer is to send more managers back to the school-yard to "unlearn" what they know, coach a team to relearn the rules, or visit the children's section of the public library to re-read "The Little Engine That Could" to get them back on the right track (after they have read Thidwick).

So, while reading and learning are helpful, it ultimately comes down to the manager's ability to think and act and be a leader. The good news is that the timing couldn't be any better. When managers are ready to lead, their people are usually equally ready to follow. To get there, leaders must be able to translate basic concepts into a unique and evolving personal philosophy which produces consistently sound judgment under the rigors of their daily organizational reality. However, even after they finally "arrive," leaders must remain continually worthy of their positions by honestly and effectively relating to their followers, and by remaining relevant to their organizations.

"The Road Not Taken" Makes All The Difference

By now, it should be clear that until managers take self-directed action to break away from their emotional and organizational "paper handcuffs" by daring to be different, they will not become muralistic leaders—the visionary risk takers—who create evolutionary changes within the organizational strategy to produce the better widget. The critical moment of truth occurs at their personal crossroads of conscious competence and conscious conformity.

Robert Frost provided the perfect metaphor in his poem, "The Road Not Taken." When managers reach the fork in their career path, they can either follow the parade down the safe and familiar route along Main Street, or head down a less familiar road to find new answers to old questions. The decision to take the road less traveled is usually less comfortable, but often makes all the difference. Indeed, it's what makes managers different. It helps them to become leaders.

In muralist cultures, therefore, leaders are not about applying restrictive controls, or keeping everything within the lines, and everyone inside their "box." They are about providing the creative license for their lifters and producers to passionately accept an increasingly higher degree of personal risk to be "different," and to be liberated to challenge their personal limits to achieve organizational goals and to ascend to higher levels of professional self fulfillment.

Conversely, it's also about setting the tone, and sending a different message to leaners. Managers who wait to be specifically directed to act, or who refuse to execute to the measure of their responsibilities, actually face an even greater risk—being replaced by others who understand the sport of business, who can show what they have done, and who have the confidence and "the look" to tell the story of how they made the difference.

Leaders Look Better When Their Followers Look Good

While there is no shortage of managers eager to be viewed as leaders, too few will graduate from the "leadership candidate school." This is another part of the leadership paradox. Individual qualities are not enough. For example, ambition alone is not the means to become a leader, because ambition by itself tends to be self-centered, inner focused, and often creates doubt, suspicion, and distrust among followers.

It's not just about great intelligence either, because a fancy college and a high IQ can quickly be misrepresented as intellectual elitism to which most people cannot relate, and quickly reject. Besides, a lot of people are "smart."

Becoming a leader also cannot be just about being a hard worker either, because hard work alone does not ensure success, let alone leadership.

Instead, leading requires a holistic set of skills—and values—not the least of which is an understanding that leading is as much about those being led as it is about those who want to lead, if not more. Nor is leadership a job for life. It is a special privilege earned only by those who are able to develop a personal leadership style through which they are able to continually communicate their philosophy and vision to their followers that evokes their passion, and sustains their confidence and trust.

The symbiotic connection between leaders and their followers is a key reason why muralism works. Within this environment, leaders remain relevant by continually raising the performance bar, challenging conventional wisdom and increasingly expanding the limits of their capabilities to produce exceptional results.

The biggest fear in muralistic cultures is the fear of letting each other down. When this happens, it's magic!

Muralism As A Form
Of Organizational Commencement

Muralism, therefore, is far more than the end result of a cultural revolution that concludes with the ascension of a charismatic leader. To have a lasting organizational legacy, the commitment to muralism must be viewed like commencement—the beginning of a new management philosophy.

The ultimate reward for muralists is the extent to which their legacy remains relevant to their organizations after they're gone. This legacy is what separates "charismatics" from muralists. The legacy of the former is focused on the individual and generally limited to the time of their involvement. Muralism is more organizationally focused and longer lasting because it is more about the culture than the personality.

As a result, an essential element of leading is preparing successors to not only sustain the level of organizational performance, but to continue to elevate it to higher levels under subsequent leadership. One critical measure of success, therefore, is the direction of an organization following a muralist's promotion or departure. If the organization subsequently fails in the absence of its "charismatic leader," or falls dramatically from prior levels of success, the muralist will have personally succeeded but organizationally failed.

Another essential element of muralism is the muralist's role as mentor-leader. By carefully mentoring, then "deputizing" their lifters to move into other parts of the organization, muralists ensure their legacy, while moving the broader organization forward, by spreading their philosophy and management culture at a much faster rate than possible by a single leader.

Think about it within this context—if one small child picking up a starfish can make a difference, what even greater things can a muralist and a group of true believers achieve?

In the end, as most things are, it's up to you. Time is wasting, so why not get started today?

The Final Word

As you make your ascent from manager to muralist and mentor-leader, keep these 12 points in mind:

1. To lead is a privilege earned, not an entitlement owed.
2. Communicate your vision very clearly, very quickly, and very often.
3. Know the difference between assets and resources.
4. People want to be led, not managed, by leaders they trust.
5. Good people are not attracted to bad leaders.
6. Remain relevant to your people and the organization.
7. Put your name on your door.
8. Promote your lifters.
9. Understand your role in the "sport" of business.
10. Your persistence must exceed their resistance.
11. Leading is about both the bold colors and the subtle tones.
12. Dare to be different.

Most of all, remember that leading requires your sustained effort, because...***You Don't Get To Be A 12-Point Buck By Luck!***

About the Author

James A. Hatherley holds a BA degree from the University of Massachusetts in Amherst, has earned several professional designations, and has also completed Executive Development training at Wharton. Nevertheless, he refers to his days at the renowned Boston Latin School as his most meaningful formal learning experience. The every-day-for-six-years requirement of translating abstract Latin text into conversational English provided him with the training and the skill for translating abstract stories and everyday events, lessons from children's books and video games, the intricacies of lily pads, and Swiss watches—even hacksaws, poached eggs, gymnastics, and garden mums—into everyday business context.

In his more than twenty-five year career as a manager and leader, from front line supervisor to general manager and corporate officer, Jim has developed *and* implemented insightful, unique, and practical leadership theories that motivate employees to excel and to deliver exceptional results by liberating them to challenge their personal limits.

In *Daring to Be Different: A Manager's Ascent to Leadership*, Jim combines his experience, business wisdom, comical narrative, and an interesting metaphorical writing style with useful leadership tools to produce a business gem. Where else can aspiring managers turn to understand how the lessons learned from the stories of an inn keeper's concerns about a 12-point buck, an artist's theory about bold colors and subtle tones, and a fraternity brother's inability to execute in a key moment are essential elements to their professional development in becoming a leader?

James Hatherley is a senior vice president of a Fortune 150 Company with more than 14.5 billion dollars in revenue and more than 37,000 employees.

Caricature by Paul Szep, twice awarded a Pulitzer Prize for editorial cartoons.